Me,
You,
and
GOD

George Edmonson

Me, You, and GOD

Group Experiments for Christians

WORD BOOKS, Publisher
Waco, Texas

First Printing—July 1973
Second Printing—March 1974

Library of Congress catalog card number: 73-76254
Printed in the United States of America

To the incredible people of Liberty . . .

Contents

Preface

I confess to as many ego needs as the next guy. Early in my Christian life I tried to deny such needs, but I find they are still there. I don't want Christ to have died for "good old what's his name." I have a need to be recognized as a person.

The bugaboo of my life has always been criticism. I have done many things and done many of them well, but always underlying any accomplishment was the fear of criticism. A life of "justification by accomplishment" in order to avoid criticism is a no-life.

My release from this no-life began to come about in 1962 through a small group experience in Germany while in the Army. This was my first introduction to caring Christians who accepted me as I was. There was no criticism, nothing to be accomplished to gain their approval. They simply loved me because they were comfortable in being loved by God themselves, and they wanted to pass it on. In this fellowship I first learned that Christ loves me as I am, not as I should be. Such a transforming experience was one that I have been absolutely unable to do without since. To me, a small group is not a "technique." It is a living experience of the incarnation of God's love without which I cannot live!

During the last ten years, I have investigated every suggestion I could find concerning the improvement of small groups. I have read every book, listened to every workshop, and questioned every experimenter that I could find. Like a man dying of thirst, I was trying to quench an insatiable thirst for more information. I had to find out about the various manifestations of the family to which I had come to belong through the brotherhood of Christ.

Through this Christian family, primarily that of Faith at Work, I have been able to grow as a human being secure in the love of Christ, but only within the last year have I been able to deal with my old nemesis, the fear of criticism. At the Faith at Work Leadership Institute in Green Lake, Wisconsin, in the fall of 1971, my brothers in the Spirit loved me into the discovery that rather than being criticized, I was living in the fearful anticipation of criticism. Expecting it so keenly, I would look around until I found something suggestive of it, seize upon it, and react as if deliberately and maliciously criticized.

The writing of *Me, You, and God* was a twofold experience for me. It was a report to those who have given me life in Christ through their love as to how the sum total of all their efforts is being lived out in the changed lives within the small groups of my own church. Secondly, it was intended to be a living encouragement to others to begin to live out their authenticity and humanness with trust in God. As far as I am able to be in touch with my own ego needs, I do not think it was "justification by accomplishment," nor was there any sense of "look what I have done." The book was simply "good news" shared with those who helped bring it about and with those who have not yet heard about such "good news."

In the fall of 1971, I heard Keith Miller speak at Earlham College. He did not know it, of course, but he had been a voice crying from my own wilderness of inauthenticity, inviting me into a new land. He had become in a sense my "spiritual father," probably more important to me than he should have been. At this lecture, he described his own convictions about small groups to a group of clergy. I was bursting with good feelings and, I am sure, no little pride, because so many of the things he described were the things we had been practicing over the last five years.

I wrote Keith and asked him to read the manuscript of *Me, You, and God*. I was relatively confident that he would like it because of all his views it shared. I waited with keen anticipation for his reply, hoping for that pat on the head my ego craved and that I so dearly wanted.

Instead, when the reply came, it left me bewildered. The book was good, but there was *too* much of Keith Miller in it. After many explanations, I came to realize that most of the crops I had harvested were traceable to hybrid seeds Keith had developed. Like the man in Mark 4:26–32, I had seen seed sprouting and growing, knowing not how, or really thinking it mattered. Suddenly, I found that Keith had planted most of that seed, and that he had intended to comply with pressure to write a book of his own concerning both its nature and its growth. Keith told me that he needed a few days to think over the whole situation and to pray and agonize over his decision.

At that point, I was more than glad that the whole problem as to what should happen to the book was his, not mine. My problem was not with the book, but with myself; whether or not I had really changed as a person. Would I again seek to feel criticized or see the dilemma honestly? In what was a world's speed record for me, I dealt with active butterflies for about twenty minutes. My part of the whole thing was resolved in the choice to reaffirm my own authenticity and my warm feelings of confidence in and brotherhood with Keith as one of those who had helped me discover the freedom of being me: it was simply to wait confidently for Keith's decision. Since then, however, increased perspective has allowed me to see that my own limited understanding of the options would have been defeating both to my authenticity and to Keith's. They would have represented George's willingness to make things right, not God's will to right things. I could have thrown the book away, given it away, or rewritten it. Any of those choices would have been the old up-tight me doing what he thought he should, not what he chose to do in the freedom of Christ. By the same token, it would have left Keith in the artificial position of "spiritual father" and would have left out a creating God completely.

Only Keith knows the struggles and agonizing he had to do, and the ways in which he had to come to grips with his own personhood. When we finally met face to face to resolve the problem, he had a proposal to offer. He could honestly affirm the value of what the book had to say about our own experiences because they had roots in his own experimentation and origination. The first part of his proposal was that the preface tell the story of what had happened to us, that there be a "living out" of the same stark honesty and simple vulnerability that had turned me on to a whole new way of life in the first place. Through the story of our own humanness, my ego needs would be met, Keith would be a brother in Christ rather than a "spiritual father," and the Spirit of God would be free to move about his people in a new and fresh way. The second part of his proposal was that a third of any royalties be designated for the work of Faith at Work, the "experimental farm" within which he had done so much planting and within which I had done so much harvesting. I was not merely "satisfied" with his suggestions, but truly excited about them. I suppose there may be something here akin to the wonder described by mothers who experience natural childbirth. Not only has something happened, but we have witnessed the powerful moving of God's unpredictable Spirit!

Acknowledgments

We owe a great debt of gratitude to the Rev. Otis E. Young for the exciting new direction afforded by the experimental method in small groups. In an article entitled, "A Reorientation to All of Life" (*Pastoral Psychology*, March 1967). Mr. Young, then the pastor of the Evangelical United Church of Christ in Webster Grove, Missouri, later the General Secretary of the Division of Church Extension of the United Church Board for Homeland Ministries, and now the senior minister of First-Plymouth Congregational Church, Lincoln, Nebraska, shared his own original experimentation in this approach. He was kind enough to furnish us with a set of the experiments he was using. We have used and modified many of his experiments and devised many of our own. I regret that time has blurred the lines that would make it possible to credit him with the specific experiments he originated. Perhaps it will suffice to say that the best ones probably were devised by him, while some of the questionable ones are probably my own!

I wish to also express my gratitude to a host of people who have introduced me to the wonder of small groups: Lt. Col. Dale and Helen Stein, who started it all for me; John and Carrol Stahlman, who have lovingly shared my growing pains; Keith Miller and Bruce Larson, who have helped me become human; and a number of people who will be forever unaware of their role as funnels for Christ.

[1]
The
Experimental
Approach

CHRISTIANITY IS EMERGING from the protective cocoon it has spun around itself as a defense against its own lack of faith in a God big enough to control and develop the creation he has begun. During the pupa period, the Bible was defended and strangled by those so insecure in their own faith that they feared to let the Bible challenge them to new insights. The Bible does not need defending. It can stand alone and meet all challengers. Childish concepts of God were defended for fear he would lose stature when seen from a fresh viewpoint. God does not need defending either. The God who is truly Lord can also stand and confront all challengers.

The standard tools of science were greatly feared during these years. It was forgotten that science is also a part of God's creation. The scientific method, honestly applied, penetrates to the heart of truth, and thus to a clearer insight into the reality and nature of the living God. The experimental approach is at the heart of the scientific method. If a thing is true, it can validate itself when put to the test. We buy clothes, tires, and toothpaste by this method. Athletic teams compete on this basis. Favorite recipes are traded or discarded according to the ability of a new dish to pass the test of the experimental approach. I cannot prove the existence of love through the tools of science, but I can be convinced

15

my wife loves me by observing the evidence of that love when given an opportunity to express itself.

I have always been impressed by the story of the man born blind described in the ninth chapter of John. Jesus healed the man's blindness. The Pharisees did their best to get the newly healed man to put some type of label on Jesus. They were playing the contemporary church game. They were highly frustrated when the man refused to play the game by their rules. All he had to share was the results of the experimental approach. He had been blind. Now he could see. Jesus was the catalyst.

The experimental approach, used within the context of the small group experience, gives promise of being the most stimulating approach to effective evangelism and Christian development encountered during the present challenging peiiod in the emerging life of the Christian Church. It has proven to be the means by which the claims of the Christian faith have been translated into understandable "good news" to a generation committed to "telling it like it is." Wherever it has been tried, it has so excited those who have participated that they have spontaneously shared their excitement with others and encouraged them to try the experience. Over half the adult members of one church have participated in these experiments and brought a lethargic church to life. Agnostics have chosen to respond to Jesus Christ. The apathetic and those who had discarded their faith have caught fire. The church has become a "new wineskin," taking on a new shape as the enthusiastic bubbling presence of "turned on" Christians exerts the pressure of its response to the living Christ.

There is no instant magic inherent in the experiments suggested. By themselves, they would be only psychological gimmicks. Their effectiveness is dependent upon their use within the context of the small group experience. By the same token, the small group can also be a psychological gimmick without the context of an experimental approach. Together, they form the basis for an honest search and response to a genuinely living God. "Is there really a God?" "Can he possibly love me like I am?" "Could anyone?" These are the questions we hesitate to ask for fear of the answer.

We never really outgrow our childhood cry, "I want to do it myself!" The content of Christian education has told us what we *should* believe and what we *should* be, but it lacks the power to cause us to internalize even the truth. Consequently, the Christian life is too often an external façade. Given the right conditions, it is a convenient façade, even a satisfying one. The flaw is that if it is only a façade it lacks the power to confront life's realities. It is a lie that we find uncomfortable to live with and that eventually becomes transparently obvious to others.

On the other hand, discovery is convincing. What we have found to be true for ourselves is unshakeable. The intention of the experimental approach to the Christian life is to allow a person to discover for himself by experiment and experience the fact of Christ's continuing life among his people. This frees each person to choose the Christian life as a deliberate choice based upon his discovery of fact as opposed to claims. This choice begins with the internalization of experience and is therefore the foundation of a life-changing faith. Lives do change. It has been an awesome experience to witness the changes that have come about in the lives of persons involved in the experimental approach.

If the experimental approach is the road by which the individual travels, the small group is the vehicle by which the journey is made possible. Many readers will have been part of a deliberate small group experience. We are relational persons and God's chosen entrance into the life history of mankind was through a life relationship. We become Christians in and through relationships, not in isolation.

Most small groups seem to share a common frustration.

17

They begin well and make great strides as a group, but there comes a time when everyone asks, "What do we do now?" The excitement of being part of an accepting group gives way to a feeling that the group is dealing with superficialities and becoming predictable. Individuals settle into roles and it is almost as if the participants were following a script. I have seen this happen over and over in groups, and I am sure the reader has also. The experimental approach used in our small groups has proven to be the answer to this problem in our experience. No two groups are ever alike. Each is characterized by its own unpredictableness and by the unpredictableness of each group member. The group literally *becomes* a group as each member *becomes* a unique person to the group.

It is my hope that the reader is or will become part of a group committed to testing the experimental approach to the Christian life. You cannot become Christian by reading about it any more than you can become pregnant by reading about babies. If you have a secret yearning for a more exciting life, you may be sure many of your friends share your longing. Call a few and invite them to share the search by starting a group with you. This is the only effective means for using this book. Recognizing, however, that some readers will simply be unable to find the courage to be part of such a group immediately, I have tried to share some typical group reactions with you. If you will be faithful in attempting each experiment, even alone, perhaps you will feel a part of one of our own groups.

The group experience is designed to be a progression over a six-month period. Experiments are divided into three sections, each section requiring eight weeks for those meeting once a week. Our first eight weeks together are designed to help us achieve an increased *awareness of ourselves.* The second eight weeks help us to develop an *awareness of others.* The final eight weeks are experiments aimed at an *awareness of God.* It is truly a journey along a defined route. It is a journey as a group, and each group will experience different discoveries along the way. There is no school solution—no right or wrong. There is only a pilgrimage into the unknown with the promise of excitement as a companion.

[2]

Some
Helpful
Rules

MANY EXCELLENT BOOKS have been written concerning group
dynamics and the techniques of successful groups. I will not
repeat such material here. However, as a result of much experimentation, we have found certain group styles to be
especially helpful. Some, subject to question when first tried,
were adopted for the simple reason that they proved to work
best. It is in this spirit that they are suggested here.

1. *The group is accepting.* No one is ever corrected for
being like he is! A small group doesn't just happen because
a number of people happen to be occupying the same space.
A group comes into being when the significant world of each
of two or more persons is to some extent involved in the
significant world of the other. Our purpose is to discover
and share these significant areas. This means listening. Someone has said that to be listened to attentively is to be loved.
The group lives by exercising curiosity rather than judgment.
It draws a person out in an attempt to understand through
the eyes of the other. Quick, easy answers help no one. They
insult the intelligence of the person seeking understanding
and they kill honesty. Participants in a small group seldom
jump in, they wade in. They send up smoke signals to see if
anyone is really listening and if anyone cares. They will ven-

21

ture further only if this experimental probing indicates they will be welcomed and respected.

2. *The leader is part of the group.* The experimental approach in small groups precludes a teacher- or God-image. The leader must be as vulnerable as anyone else in the group. An unsuccessful small group can usually point to a manipulative leader. The leader must exercise certain leadership functions, but not from a privileged sanctuary. It is unfortunate that some ordained clergymen will violently refuse to become part of such a group due to fear of being known as they are by their parishioners. The creative alternative is to discover each other—complete with flaws and wonderful unseen qualities. The leader will be wise to encourage the maximum distribution of leadership among the group members. His goal should be to make himself unnecessary and replaceable in his leadership role, but needed as a person. He can do much to encourage participation and meaningful communication. The group will look to him during its early life to help create and maintain a group climate in which feelings and expressions are accepted.

3. *The group is closed.* This rule was first suggested to me several years ago by Keith Miller during a workshop on small groups. I was certain that he was a squirrel who had lost his tree! After trying the closed group, I feel this rule is imperative! Nothing of note will come from a group until each person has determined the trustworthiness and availability of every other participant. This too will be determined by experiment. Each of us has sly little ways to test others to find out if it is safe to become more transparent. There are no ground rules that can make it safe, only trial by fire. Consider then the intrusion of a stranger upon a meeting. He may have the greatest personality and the most disarming mannerisms, but he is unknown, untested. Nothing important will happen that night.

4. *We meet in homes.* Our home is part of the total expres-

sion of ourselves. Unless we meet in one another's homes, part of our work is undone. It is easy to play a game when you are a guest in someone else's home or the church hall. You can fool not only the rest of the group, but yourself as well. It is a completely different ball of wax if you have to allow the group into a home of which you are ashamed or that has become a showplace of your problem with pride. Some of our best meetings have been conducted on the floor of a small room with insufficient chairs or around a kitchen table. One of the most pathetic experiences was having a woman tell me that she was ashamed to have people in her home because it was so pretentious. She and her husband had worked and slaved a lifetime to be able to live in a house to which she was ashamed to invite guests! We encourage our hosts to allow us to share their home with them without special preparations. It is unimportant that they give it a special dusting or cleaning. Refreshments are kept simple. A plugged-in coffee pot is enough. Beginning with the second eight-week set of experiments, the host becomes our leader, the organizing leader by now having become just another member of the group. If his call is to be an enabler for such groups, he is free to leave and begin another group. The leadership function will rotate with the meeting place of the group.

5. *The group takes social priority.* We commit ourselves to the group for each eight-week block. During that eight weeks, the group involvement is the first item put on the calendar. It is inevitable that some members will be out of town on business matters or will be absent for similar reasons, but the group takes absolute social priority. Just because God comes into our lives free does not mean that there is no price to be paid. We meet on the same night of the week each week, in our case on Thursday nights. If Aunt Minnie decides to come to visit next Thursday night, she will have to entertain herself. Something of prime importance is happening that night! If the PTA decides to have an open house

that night, we will have to explain to the children that something of vast importance is happening that night. Great things happen in our groups because they are given priority and we go expectantly. It has been an astounding experience to see businessmen rearrange their calendars because of their involvement in this experience. One man, a certified public accountant just beginning his own business, turned down several badly needed accounts because they would have conflicted with the meeting of his group! Would you do as much? Do not expect anything to happen in your experimentation with the Christian life until you are willing to confront your system of priorities.

6. *If you don't do the assignment, don't come to the meeting.* Once this rule is stated to the group, it should never have to be exercised. This is a matter of attitude with which one comes to the group. There are no freeloaders. This is no more than mutual respect and an attitude of sincerity in approaching the purpose of the group. As is true with most endeavors, you get out of the group what you put into it. If one hasn't completed his assignment, he is communicating to the rest of the group members, "You aren't very important to me." The words "disciple" and "discipline" share the same root. The attempt to be an "undisciplined disciple" is a contradiction in terms. Once again, it is necessary to confront your system of priorities.

7. *Don't share the discoveries of others outside the group.* This is another rule that once stated can be forgotten, but it does need to be stated. Each member is free to share the excitement of his own discoveries outside the group all he wishes. The sharing of good news is at the heart of the Christian life. It is obviously necessary, however, to respect the confidences of others. If they wish to share their own discoveries, fine. They must be assured from the start that they are free to share any manner of thoughts and attitudes with the group and that they will remain with the group.

24

Some Helpful Rules

Nothing kills a group more quickly and more justifiably than allowing it to degenerate into a session of "bitch and snitch."
8. *Honor the time limit.* The group should decide for itself how long it is to meet. The starting time is not less than two hours and more frequently up to three hours. Once this limit is set by group decision, the leader must hold the group to it ruthlessly, at least during the first eight weeks. Some persons will have other commitments following the meeting. Baby-sitters will have to be returned home. Without the assurance that the time limit will be honored, they will hesitate to participate freely during the closing moments for fear of starting something that will drag on. Others will keep putting off the sharing of important inputs they want desperately to share. With an agreed-upon stopping time, they will be encouraged to exercise responsibility in deciding when their time has come to really get in the swim. If you find it difficult to exercise such control over the time limit, set an alarm clock for the agreed-upon time. When it sounds, quit—even in the middle of a sentence! This does not mean that everyone must leave, of course. It means that members are free to leave. The experiment for the night is over. Once a group has really become a caring group, there are nights when you can't drive them away with a stick. They will talk into the wee hours, but their continued participation is a matter of responsible choice, not entrapment.

[3]
How
Do We
Start?

THE FIRST MEETING is of utmost importance. The ability of a group of apprehensive people to meet in a comfortable and relaxed atmosphere is dependent upon the preparation of the leader. The goal of the evening is to break down the barriers separating us, to outline the direction of the group's life together, and to explain the rules that will be followed.

Refreshments should be available to the group as they arrive. There is no better place to hide one's feelings of inadequacy than behind a cup of coffee. Some persons have more successful ways of hiding feelings of inadequacies than others, but we all seem to share them. "What will people think of me?" "How will I sound?" "What am I getting into?" These thoughts will be racing through the heads behind the smiling faces. Help them to the first cup of coffee and let them know they can help themselves to a refill whenever they wish. Being waited upon only adds to any feelings of anxiety. Being free to serve yourself gives a feeling of freedom and warmth.

As soon as everyone has arrived, start without apology or disclaimer. The group may appear to be enjoying light chatter, but each person has come for a reason. It is reassuring to group members to know that the leader feels it is important and is anxious to start the adventure.

We have found a discussion starter attributed to the Quakers to be most helpful in breaking both the ice and any barriers.* It consists of a series of questions to be answered by each person in turn, beginning with the leader. The leader sets the tone of informality and honesty by his own answers. Each question is answered by all the group members before moving on to the next question.

1. *Tell us your name and where you lived between the ages of 7 and 12. If you lived in more than one place during those years, tell us about the one that stands out most in your mind. How many brothers and sisters did you have at that time?* As the group leader, allow yourself to reminisce a little about the house and your brothers or sisters. Establish an example of freedom to recall that will encourage others to recall significant memories.

2. *How did you heat your home at that time?*

3. *Where in your home at that time (perhaps a room or a person) was the center of human warmth?* This is a critical time for the leader to be honest. If you experienced the gift of human warmth, share it with the group. If you were not fortunate enough to share human warmth, be frank in saying so. You will find group members who had no experiences of human warmth during those years.

4. *Share with the group the purpose of these questions, that we are crudely tracing the human experience of security.* During our formative years, we were given a place to live and other people to live with. In the beginning, simple physical comfort was important to our security. We needed a warm place to stand on a cold morning. At some time we began to need the more important security of human warmth.

*Developed by Keith Miller. Taken from *Groups That Work*, by Walden Howard (Editor), Copyright © 1967, by Zondervan Publishing House, and used by permission. For more on group conversation technique, see *The Art of Group Conversation*, by Rachel Davis DuBois and Mew-Soong Li (New York: The Association Press, 1963).

Some found it. Some did not. We are together because we are still searching for an ultimate security. We want to find out if we can be accepted, even loved, by others. We want to find out if there is such a reality as a God capable of accepting and loving us. Does he have the ability to influence the future development of our lives?

5. *When, if ever, did God become more than a word to you, a living Being, capable of influencing your life?* Do not go around the group with this question. Throw it out to be answered by anyone wishing to do so. Don't encourage the recitation of ancient conversion experiences. Allow time for anyone wishing to answer to do so, but not so much time as to make those not wishing to respond uncomfortable.

We have developed an alternative set of warm-up questions for those of a younger generation. There is no purpose achieved by having college-age youth share that they heated their home by turning up the thermostat! You may find these questions helpful in moving toward the same objective of tracing the development of security.

1. *Describe the room you lived in during your freshman year in high school. How many brothers and sisters did you have at the time?*

2. *What one thing stands out as your most satisfying experience or success during high school?*

3. *Tell us about an experience you feel good about when you received help in some way from someone which went beyond what you could have accomplished alone.*

4. *When, if ever, has God been a personal being in your own experience, capable of giving such help?*

Now share with the group an outline of the direction your group life will take together. We have found it most helpful to have each session consist of a balance achieved by both experimentation and Bible study. Bible study serves to achieve a desirable orientation. We find ourselves being called into question rather than being our own source of au-

thority concerning life norms. During earlier attempts, we
included prayer as a third element. We found prayer to be
an unnatural and forced part of our group life. We prayed
because we were supposed to, not because of any actual value
felt by the group. A strange and wonderful thing happened
when we eliminated prayer as a normal part of the group
life. Nothing whatever was said about prayer by the leader,
but in each and every group without exception, the group
raised the question after being together for seven or eight
weeks. They would express the feeling that they were missing
something and decide by group decision to include prayer. In
many cases, the question would be raised by the very person
who was trying to convince the group that he or she was
the greatest skeptic of the group! Prayer then became an
honest part of the group life, not frosting on an otherwise
palatable cake.

1. *The Experiment.* The group is introduced to the first
experiment on Awareness of Self. Each person is asked to
read it carefully and to ask any questions at this point. It is
helpful if each person has his own book in which he may
write notes. Each person is to conduct the experiment during
the week and to return the following week prepared to discuss his findings with the group. It is stressed that we are
looking for a new viewpoint concerning ourselves, not new
information.

2. *The Bible Study.* This early moment in the group's life
is not the time for democratic action in determining the Bible
passage to be studied. All are more comfortable with an assignment rather than a decision. We have used a special
approach during the first eight weeks that is not continued
beyond that time. We have arbitrarily selected the Book of
Philippians for study. Each person is to *write* a *paraphrase*
of a given portion in his own words. A "churchy" vocabulary
is to be avoided. Each person writes the portion in his own
way with words and phrases meaningful to him. We have

shared fantastically meaningful thoughts complete with the common slang of our own generation. The use of paraphrase kills superstition toward the Bible at its inception and allows the meaning to find fresh expression. Each person is told that when he comes back next week, he will read his paraphrase without comment and then summarize in one sentence what *he* felt was the chief idea. Each person will follow this procedure in turn. After all have been heard, the question before the house will be, "So what?" We are not interested in commentaries and historical backgrounds. We are only concerned with what the Bible says to our situation here and now! The Bible does not have to be defended by the leader. God's Word can stand by its own power. A part of the experimental approach is to share an honest search for the answer to the question, "So what?"

I have included my own first attempts at paraphrase. There is nothing to commend or distinguish these paraphrases other than their own crudeness. No attempt has been made to dress them up for purpose of publication. The chief idea listed was the first one to occur. There is no attempt at theological sophistication. I am sure that the reader can improve upon both the paraphrase and the idea engendered, and it is my hope that you will take the time to do so.

Once discussion starts, whether on the experiment or the Bible passage, it is sometimes difficult to curtail. We attempt to give half of our time to each. In order to avoid becoming mechanical, we alternate the one we start with each week. If we begin with the experiment this week, we will begin with the Bible study the next week. Thus, if an especially fruitful discussion is under way, there is no obligation to end it simply to move on to another task.

We have correlated the passages in Philippians with the experiments on Awareness of Self as follows:

Experiment #1: Philippians 1:1–18
Experiment #2: Philippians 1:19–30
Experiment #3: Philippians 2:1–13
Experiment #4: Philippians 2:14–30
Experiment #5: Philippians 3:1–11
Experiment #6: Philippians 3:12–21
Experiment #7: Philippians 4:1–23

When the group is prepared to begin the second set of experiments, Awareness of Others, it can itself determine the book it wishes to study. A more traditional approach to study will be in order by then.

Without exception, each group will experience a "magic night" when the group really gels as a group. It cannot be predicted, but the group will know when it happens. It usually happens about the sixth or seventh week. It will be a night when acceptance of one another and a feeling of responsibility for one another becomes such a reality that members will go home talking about it. It will be a night when the leader loses much of his night's sleep from the excitement he feels. There will be other tough nights to face, but they will be influenced by the night when the group "happened." For those readers who are beginning the group experience, good luck as you begin an adventure you will never forget. The living God is with us!

[4]
Awareness
of
Self

Experiment No. 1

Most of us like to think of ourselves as "Prince Charmings" or "Cinderellas," with nothing worse than a few harmless idiosyncrasies.

One of the first pathways to health and self-understanding is to be able to laugh at some of our own shortcomings, rather than to suppress them. If we have had practice in hiding them, it may require a real effort in self-awareness to reveal them.

This week, become aware of how you "bug" your mate, or, if you are mateless, your closest friend. Don't ask, but think and observe. What things do you do that bring a "You're bugging me!" response? How can you tell when you get this response from your mate or friend?

33

NOTES:

Awareness of Self: Experiment No. 1

Everyone approaches the first experiment in a serious attempt at self-awareness with real apprehension. It is readily apparent in some, while concealed under bluster and bravado by others. This experiment serves a valuable purpose in making it possible to exercise humor while looking at one's own faults. It is quickly discovered that we are all in the same boat. The lists are remarkably similar and it is comforting to find that you are "normal" when compared with a roomful of other people.

I wonder how many marriages have been saved, or at least materially improved, by this ridiculously simple experiment! Husbands and wives confess to one another. Until this time, each had assumed he or she was the only one "bugged" by certain actions of the other. Now, each discovers that both the victim and perpetrator have suffered to some extent from whatever the action may have been. One was offended or annoyed, but the other was left feeling guilty. Now that all is out on the table, they have both had a good laugh over not only the offending action, but over its unreasonably lasting effect. From this night on, over and over again, when a minor annoyance is inflicted on one mate by the other, we hear, "You're bugging me!" followed by the laughter of both. Instant medicine!

The range of male offenses extends from putting their wives down to leaving the toilet seat up. Almost all his bugging actions are those that are deflating to the female ego. Either the man appears to be inconsiderate, or he is elevating his own self-confidence at the expense of his wife. Some men find their stature by using their wives as pedestals! If both can laugh at this tendency, a tremendous obstacle has been removed to the happiness of both.

The "bugging" done by wives, coincidentally, is almost always a threat to the male ego. Even a toothpaste tube can be a battleground when the wife is an erratic "squeezer" and the husband a systematic "roller." We have a sad situation where both the man and woman need desperately to be affirmed by their mate as acceptable just as they are. Yet each appears to act from self-censure in reducing the stature of the other without deliberately intending to do so. You can become taller by growing higher or by reducing the size of all others around you. This seems to be an unconscious tendency of so many of us who would deny its truth to our last gasping breath. List for yourself the ways in which you "bug" your mate or closest friend, and check yourself to see if you too might be an offender.

My most embarrassing discovery as a member of a group was to discover that I did not really want to do this assignment. I knew I bugged my wife, but I didn't really want to find out how! My list was as mercifully short as a somewhat manipulated memory could make it. It ran something like this:

1. Having to be right. I not only think I'm right when we disagree on something, but have to prove to my wife where she's wrong for her own education!

2. Poking into food, especially baked foods, before they're done. I hate to have anyone see something I'm making before it's completely done, but I don't see why she's that way! Any husband who hasn't dipped a finger into the cookie batter just hasn't lived!

3. Deciding for her. When out for a drive, for example, I may ask her if she wants to stop for an ice cream cone. That sounds good to me, but she wants to be invited to stop for a snack of her own choosing, not one chosen from my list for her.

4. Precise punctuality. If I am supposed to be at a meeting at a specific time, I may be fifteen minutes early, but never a second late. If we are going someplace together, or as a family, the same applies. I carry this to ridiculous extremes in leaving for sporting events or even just for drives. If the agreed departure time is four o'clock, I

don't mind leaving early, but if everyone isn't in the car on the stroke of four, I am the one having the next stroke!

My wife and I have laughed over these "bugging" actions and many others. They no longer threaten us, even if they sometimes return to haunt our relationship. We are able to find our security from mutual affirmation, rather than through self-manufactured compensations.

More rare, but far more serious, are those offenses described by an occasional group member as being reasonable and normal retaliation against a mate. Such a person sees nothing humorous about this experiment. Typically, it is a man who describes himself in these terms. He blusters his way into the meeting with explanations that he is there only because of his wife. He is loud and tries to sidetrack meaningful, and therefore threatening, discussions. When he jokes, it is with biting satire. When his turn comes to participate in this experiment, he is anxious to tell how he "bugs" his wife. He begins by describing her shortcomings, and explains how he "naturally" reacts in certain ways which bug her. It is thereby her fault that she is bugged, not his! As an example, he may tell of a dinner party his wife prepared. He thought the roast was too well done and made quite an issue of it in front of the guests. He then clarifies his presentation by explaining that sometimes he has bugged his wife by criticizing her cooking, "but it's her own fault."

Such a man is both a test and an opportunity for a small group. It would be very simple to point out his faults to him and to make him feel both unacceptable and unaccepted. In truth, his actions probably stem from his own certainty that there is something unacceptable about him. Further condemnation will not allow an unthreatened self-examination and chosen change. The task of the group is a simple one. We want first to be certain we understand the man. We listen to him carefully and ask such questions as are necessary to clarify what he has said. We want to understand what he has said through his own eyes. Secondly, we accept him as he is. No one points out his assumed shortcomings. If he has to make us understand clearly how he sees himself in relationship with his wife, you may be certain that he also clearly understands! After all, he was eavesdropping while he was telling us.

It is also important that we discuss the reaction of our victim mate that signals a fifteen-yard penalty for "bugging." The signals fall into one of two clear categories. Either things get deadly quiet, or there is an immediate eruption. Our built-in antennas never miss the signal!

We have spent a lot of time discussing which reaction is most helpful. It would seem that the silent treatment is non-communicative. This then serves no useful purpose. On the other hand, an immediate eruption sometimes signals a battle for survival of status. Fortunately, the quickly discovered "You're bugging me!" response offers a natural solution. It is like saying, "That hurts me!" and immediately calling off the game. In the unconscious attempt for stature, the offender has seldom been aware that he was inflicting pain. When he becomes aware of it, he usually chooses to desist. As in an act of chivalry, both are affirmed.

In the pursuit of awareness of self, it is comforting to find that we are really all very much alike and that our actions are rather normal. It gives us courage to continue the group experience, and even a tingle of excitement.

Paraphrase No. 1
(Philippians 1:1–18)

From Paul and Timothy, a couple of Christians, to all the committed Christians in Philippi, both chiefs and Indians: Hi!

Boy, every time I think of you characters, I have to thank God. Working for Christ with you has been a blast, and I'm sure there's more yet to come. You can't imagine how much this close relationship continues to mean to me, especially since I have been thrown into the jug and can't see you in person. God knows how much I wish I could be back sharing your lives with you. I continue to pray that you will grow more and more as Christians, and that God will cap off your own strivings toward love in your lives by making you more like him daily.

Would you believe it? Throwing me in the hoosegow has backfired on them and has actually done more for Christianity than my preaching was doing! It has been a witness to everyone here, even Caesar's own guards. Others are finding more courage to witness than ever before.

Some of the preaching is aimed at knifing me in the back, but others are faithful. The faithful are showing love and understanding toward the necessity of my being here if I am to be a faithful witness. Others think I'm sort of a fanatical nut for not going along with their way of being a Christian.

I couldn't care less as long as people are finding out about Christ. That's what I'm happy about!

Chief idea to me: Confidence and optimism in what is basically a pessimistic situation.
Chief idea to you?

So what?

[5]

Awareness
of
Self

Experiment No. 2

WHAT IS THE PURPOSE of your life? What are you living for?
Why do you want to keep on living? What is the meaning of
your existence? Are you striving toward short range and long
range goals?

Our lives are frequently "fuzzy" because our answers to
the above questions are also "fuzzy." General answers, "To
help others," "To find fulfillment," "To be happy," "To be
successful," are inadequate answers. What are the measuring
sticks by which such answers become meaningful? Recognizing such specific measuring sticks and stating them will
help us clarify our lives and give a vast new insight into our
own existence.

Think about these questions and come prepared next week
to tell us what your purposes and goals are. Be specific!!

NOTES:

This experiment is deceptively difficult! For many persons, the concept of setting goals and working toward them in specific measurable ways is foreign. For others, the technique of goal-setting has become so mechanical that life has lost its mystery. In the group setting, it is helpful for each person to examine his own process of goal-setting against his flexibility in being able to respond to the unexpected. It is possible to miss the forest because of the trees, but it is equally possible to miss the forest because of not going to the place trees can be found. In other words, mechanical goal-setting may obscure a genuine opportunity for the movement of life into an unexpected direction. On the other hand, purposelessness is essentially life-retarding.

We have experienced exciting results from this experiment. Several persons have chosen totally different life styles, even new occupations. As they discussed their thoughts, many revealed that most of their important life decisions were not really decisions at all, but capitulations to existing circumstances. Once this fact has been discovered, there has been an almost universal tendency to embrace life as a God-given gift. The individual has discovered that he is a free man— free to decide and to choose his future.

One man revealed a frustration with his job. It was a well-paying position with an apparently secure future, but was not satisfying to him. It did not fulfill any purpose other than security for his family. As he talked, he revealed that if he were really to choose his own future he would enter a completely different profession. His wife excitedly chimed in by saying that this new profession was precisely the one she had always secretly hoped he would enter. Needless to say, he made the switch. His life now has a purpose that was lacking previously. As a footnote to this illustration, the company for whom this man had worked, a branch plant of an industrial giant employing several thousand men, has just announced as of this writing that it is closing its local plant!

One can't help but speculate on the relationship between goal-setting, freedom of choice, and the fingerprints of God!

Another man expressed a long-standing desire to go into business for himself. His wife appeared to be so obsessed by the need for security as to make such a change difficult, if not impossible. In a surprise move, having nothing to do with his professional competence, his position was deleted from his employer's work force and he was on his own. He is now in his own business and making a success of it.

In finding the purpose of one's life, it is not the profession of belief, but the internalization of belief, that is the effector. Faith is linked to that which is internalized, not that which is verbalized. This experiment can be a significant one in your life if you conduct it at a gut level. Only you know the difference between what is true and what you want others to think is true. This is your experiment. You are concerned with the awareness of yourself. What is true?

Paraphrase No. 2
(Philippians 1:19–30)

I am happy because I am sure that between your prayers for me and the help of Christ's living working presence, everything is going to turn out O.K. Christ will come out on top in respect to my life whether I live or am killed. If they let me live, it is a witness to Christ. If they kill me, that is better yet from my standpoint. I'm not even sure which I prefer. If they let me live, I can put my life to good work for Jesus Christ. As far as I'm concerned, I would just as soon they kill me and free me to live with Christ right now. However, I think it is necessary for me to continue living for awhile for your good, not mine. I think this will still help you in your Christian growth.

One thing though—whether I'm with you or not—live as

true Christians! The quality of your lives will defeat your enemies. They will see that we are not Christians because we think it will give us an easier life, but that we accept anything they throw at us with the courage of Christ himself.

Chief idea to me: Death is not the end so is not the ultimate threat!
Chief idea to you?

So what?

[6]

Awareness
of
Self

Experiment No. 3

If you are truly aware of yourself, you will know what you are most afraid of. We must confront our basic fears in order to improve our present level of self-awareness.

This week, recall again what you are afraid of. As you go through each day this week, think about your fears. Make a list of the things you find you are afraid of each day in addition to others that come to mind.

What are the physical sensations of your fears? How do you know you are afraid?

NOTES:

Some people state that they have no fears, only anxieties. They then begin listing a series of crippling anxieties. It is the crippling nature of fear that concerns us, whether we admit to fear or prefer to think only in terms of anxieties. An exploration of awareness of self must include a look at crippling fears. When a person is crippled by fear, he is for that period of time under less than full self-control. He is like an athlete with a pulled hamstring. He may look the part and even be going through the proper actions at the proper place. However, if put to the test, it will be quickly seen that he is not functioning adequately. The starting place for an athlete is admitting to the coach that he is hurt. The starting place for a person is to admit to himself where he is crippled.

As we have shared long lists of fears, we have noticed that without exception they contained this element of the power to cripple. They always included the inability of a person to function adequately as master of the situation. A person with a fear of snakes, for instance, would not feel the same fear when looking at snakes behind glass in a zoo. It is the element of being suddenly confronted with a snake in unexpectedly close proximity that petrifies. The snake becomes the controller of the situation and the fearful person becomes only a terrified observer.

This same point is emphasized by the physical sensations of fear. Each represents an abnormal physical functioning. Quite often it includes a temporary feeling of paralysis. "Scared stiff" is an appropriate expression of fact for many people.

When mutual acceptance within the group has become a reality, another type of fear is usually expressed. Someone will timidly say that he is afraid of meeting strangers or expressing himself in a group for fear of sounding foolish. This brings an avalanche of company! It seems that we are almost without exception fearful of being rejected. Here is a real crippler! We control ourselves and, to avoid rejection,

49

become something other than we are. Maybe this would make sense if we were the only peculiar apple in the barrel, but we find out quickly we are all this way. We all need the freedom simply to be what we are and to be accepted on that basis alone. The amazing thing is that if we can be ourselves and risk rejection on that basis, we are overwhelmingly accepted. It is the false and phony within us that is seen through and rejected. Our genuine nature, complete with weaknesses, when shared, gains us acceptance.

Another response has been so frequent as to deserve notice. Many persons, particularly women, have a great fear of becoming a burden to someone in their old age. Some are persons who have had to deal with the agonizing problems relating to the care of loved ones no longer able to care for themselves. In many ways, this too is a problem of low self-esteem. We have seen persons expressing the greatest capacity of love in caring for aged persons, but fearful of being too great a burden upon their own children. It seems that at least some fear of not being loved complicates such a problem. This is a fear of rejection based on health or age. If we have learned to love and to be loved, the facts of health and age are only the data of a person's life, not the nature of the person. This may not appear to be a crippling fear on the surface, but it may well be. Attempts may be made to "deserve" the love of children in advance. Others may reject such love now in order to "draw upon it" at a later time—like an unused savings account. Still others may live their most productive and potentially enjoyable years in isolation, amassing a substantial financial estate to be reserved for their last years. For still others, every new gray hair is cause for panic and the stimulus for psychotherapy.

At this point, talk of a God who keeps a head count on his sparrows and tally of the hairs on one's head is meaningless verbalization. It simply cannot be internalized. God's concern will be communicated only through and after the acceptance of the group. This is incarnation theology in action—God working in and through man. This is the time for sharing both fear and acceptance. This is the time to say to your new-found friend, "You nut! You're afraid of the same things I'm afraid of, and I am beginning to feel comfortable with you."

Paraphrase No. 3
(Philippians 2:1–13)

If we expect things to look up because of Christ—if we are allowing him to live in our place and give us the boost of being loved and being able to love—then let's get together so that our actions and attitudes are like one person. That means we start thinking of the other guy first instead of ourselves.

We ought to be like Jesus. He had every right to lord it over us because he was the essence of life in human form, but he chose to live his life just like we have to, and even went further and lived it out like a real social reject has to. He kept it up even though it got him killed. Because of this, the same intelligent creating power that has given us life has made the life and person of Jesus the most important thing in the world.

That's why you shouldn't be too cocky about getting out of predicaments. Wake up and realize that God is working out a plan. Your job is to obey, just like Christ did, whether things are going your way or not—so get with it!

Chief idea to me: Obeying God faithfully, rather than manipulation, is the key to life's rough spots.

Chief idea to you?

So what?

[7]
Awareness
of
Self

Experiment No. 4

IF SOMEONE COULD give you one day to do anything you wished, what would you do during that twenty-four hours? There is no money limit imposed; you can travel to any point on the earth to begin the day; there are no hindering responsibilities.

Also this week, do something that you have always wanted to do or hoped to do, but just never got around to. Whether little or large, do it!

Start early on this assignment so that it gets done. Come prepared next week to report to the rest of the group on this assignment.

NOTES:

Awareness of Self: Experiment No. 4

Does a man need a dream? It seems that every business executive has a bit of vagabond hidden within him. If it weren't for a chain of restricting circumstances, he sometimes thinks he would like just to loaf on the beach of a deserted island, dive for sunken treasure, or sail a ketch around the world. I would suspect that there are beachcombers who indulge in fantasy and imagine themselves the president of some giant industrial firm, pushing buttons and shouting orders.

Deep within every man is a tiny seed of doubt about the nature of his daily life. Some men confront the doubt and choose a radically different life style. Other men entomb the doubt in a petrified forest of "duty," living a life of mounting frustration and resentment. By far the vast majority of us simply laugh off our tiny seed of doubt as if it were part of a child's Walter Mitty world. It is an idle daydream that neither confronts nor subdues us.

The Christian is a free man. The Christian life style is one of responsible freedom. Man is responsible only to God. He is not required by the fact of his creation to become part of the machinery of a conventional society. He is a steward of his own life and is responsible only to God for an accounting of his faithfulness. We are not entitled to the luxury of passing judgment on the relative worth of a human being as he lives out a chosen life style that reflects where he is with his Lord. God alone knows the motivation that sends a man to a cloistered cell, a Wall Street business office, or a hospital tent in Lambaréné. The only sin is that the question is often never asked. The idle daydream is not confronted.

This experiment allows us to dream in a specific way. What would we do with twenty-four hours if the sky was the limit? We are free because it is only a dream. We have to be specific because of the nature of the experiment. With this measure of freedom and compulsion, we are helped to confront the hidden doubts about our present life style.

55

In order to avoid losing ourselves in a philosophical hash consisting only of words about words, we have to do something specific. The second part of the experiment is all-important! We promise to indulge ourselves in some way, however small. It has been said that every man needs the target of an unfulfilled dream throughout his life. I think it more probable that he needs a memory full of spoiled targets —targets with bull's-eyes riddled with the fact of accomplished hopes. Since we have to act, we deal with our dreams and find the true measure of their elusive power to satisfy. There is no power in merely reading about this experiment. Do it yourself! Let your experience be the data upon which you determine your conclusions.

It is inevitable that at least one person in each group finds he is "too busy" during the week to complete the second part of the experiment. He is unable to indulge himself in the accomplishment of even one small hope. If we are that busy, we are much busier than God intends! If our occupations are that restricting, chances are our attitude toward the meaning of being employed is all wrong.

This experiment is one of my favorites. It is a delight to do and a pleasure to share with others. It tells us much about ourselves and the world in which we live. I have been impressed with the desire to escape contained in the responses. I have dealt primarily with suburban people. They are living out an escapist sociology even in their choice of residence. I would be curious to see if their inner-city counterparts were also obsessed with escape, perhaps even more so.

The desire for escape we have experienced in our groups is not escape from a place, but from pressure. The men in our groups, almost without exception, opt for a place free of people. It may be a lake in Switzerland, a deserted island, or a sailing ship, but it is basically devoid of people. The activity described is less significant. It is sometimes placid and sometimes furiously active. Whatever the activity, it is a brand new adventure. It would appear that it is not the physical activity that bothers men, but the human relationships. We find ourselves right at the point of the purpose of our group as a group.

The women in our groups have indicated a different nature. Two trends have shown up, but both have a basic similarity. Many women choose to stay right at home, but without the demands of the home. They want to call in a cleaning woman to transform their home so that they can find time to dress for dinner in a romantic setting with their husbands. We men certainly take our wives for granted when it comes to the drudgery of home maintenance.

The other conspicuous trend was toward the revisiting of some place which had proven delightful in the past. This revisit usually includes the sharing of this special spot with chosen friends. There seems to be a desire to expand experiences, but within what is felt to be safe limits. The basic similarity of both groups of women is that they stay close to home and its emotional security. While the husband is tempted to pick up stakes and move to Tibet, his wife is hoping to make the nest more comfortable right where it is.

The acted-out part of this experiment has been tremendously interesting. Some persons have chosen to do something that is related to their twenty-four hour fantasy. Others have appeared to be totally nonrelated. The biggest struggle seems to be that of simply taking yourself seriously enough to do whatever is planned. You find that the world isn't shocked from its orbit. Few, if any, even notice. Consider the man who decides to sleep late. He goes to bed with something akin to conspiratorial glee. He is sure the business will collapse without him. The next morning his wife gets up and he rolls over and goes back to sleep with a broad grin. He is on top of the world, not so much because he is sleeping late, as from a feeling of rebellion against his restrictions. This goes on for a couple of hours, and he begins to get restless. Finally he gets up. By the time he gets to the meeting of the group, he has decided it wasn't really that big a deal. He has dared to experiment and now has found a new outlook. The business did not collapse. Extra sleep is not the answer to his real frustrations. If there was a real moment of joy, it was in the moment of decision to escape from the entrapment of the routine. He can choose this any time he wishes through all sorts of means, even in the midst of his work.

Perhaps a man who has completed this experiment is ready to take a fresh look at Christianity. In Christ, nothing is ever routine! All of life is an adventure into the unexpected. It is just what men crave. Men have largely abdicated from the church and its system of "religion" in recent years. Small wonder. Religion has become emasculated and security-centered. "Let me hide myself in thee," says a favorite hymn. The distortion of Christianity into something referred to by someone as the experience of the "upper womb" cannot be that initiated by the manhood of Jesus. Our Lord attracted and excited men. It is time to discard the depiction of an unexciting man, dressed in a robe that looked like a long dress and carrying a lamb, and recover the athletic figure of a bronzed man striding through the mountains in the free fulfillment of his destiny!

Paraphrase No. 4
(Philippians 2:14–30)

Don't gripe like everybody else these days. Let the quality of your life in God stand out in their midst like a sore thumb. If my life will accomplish nothing more than lead you to a full experience of God, I'll be happy enough. You do the same.

I hope I can send Timothy to you pretty soon to bring

back news from you. Timothy has been like my own son to me. I don't know anyone else other than him who shares my real concern for you. Most of the people here are too busy looking after themselves first. I'll send him as soon as I have some idea what is going to happen to me. I hope I'll be free to come also soon.

I thought I should send Epy back to you. He's been my brother and real Christian worker here. He has been anxious to get back to you and was sorry to hear that you knew of his sickness. He was extremely sick and almost bought the farm, but God brought him through, as much for my sake as his, I'm sure. I'll miss him, but I'm sending him back so that you may celebrate his return. He deserves a warm welcome, for he nearly died in carrying out your mission to me in Christian love.

Chief idea to me: Faithfulness in the midst of unfaithfulness.

Chief idea to you?

So what?

[8]

Awareness
of
Self

Experiment No. 5

THIS WEEK, as you meet people, try to discover what you dislike about them. What irritates you the most about some person in particular or a number of persons in general. Why do you think you dislike these traits or characteristics?

NOTES:

At first glance, this may appear to be an experiment about other people. If you will conduct it carefully, you will discover some things about yourself. No individual is deliberately an irritating person. He is like he is because it makes sense to him. His life style is either satisfying to him or aimed at gaining satisfaction. There is no universal rule that judges him as a person to be disliked by all. The judgment is in the eye of the beholder. By examining the things we find annoying, we will gain a new viewpoint concerning the person annoyed, namely, ourselves.

I would rather hide my own discoveries concerning this experiment under a cloak of editorial anonymity. However, conclusions applying to other people in this experiment must be drawn very carefully. The valuable discoveries are the ones a person makes about himself. I can only share a few of my own gripes about others and the corresponding revelations about myself and hope you will grant their validity for me alone. You will have a completely different list. I would suggest that you could compile valid revelations about yourself that correspond to your list.

I will spare you (and myself) from a long list, but these are exemplary:

1. I am irritated by people who fail to be prompt in keeping appointments. I have already shared my obsession with promptness in the first experiment. There is no excuse for foisting this foible upon others. If I am willing to pay the price, I can always cancel their appointments and move on to other pressing business. I am not willing to pay the price. I would rather be annoyed. In secret, I envy those who are not strangled by time-consciousness. I even find it difficult to camp in the wilds of Canada on vacation without an accurate watch. Would the world end if I ate at an odd time or started fishing a half hour later than intended? It is my problem, not that of others.

2. I dislike people who are deliberately rude. This seems to be a safe judgment. I can assume you will not find this unusual. Yet, I see something about myself through this complaint. I have often wanted to really tell someone off. Frankly, there are times when I feel they really have it coming. Nevertheless, because of my self-enforced concept of the Christian role, I normally refrain. I envy those who can genuinely react as persons at a given point in a situation without regard to an assumed role. The line between rudeness and frankness is one we draw ourselves according to our involvement in the situation. If I hurt you, I am being frank. If you hurt me, I will accuse you of being rude!

3. I am irritated by people who agree to do a particular job and then make no attempt whatsoever to be competent in carrying it out. I am a perfectionist. If I cut logs for a fireplace, they will all be the same size. If I am conducting a meeting, I will be there long ahead of time to arrange the room. My shop is lined with tools hanging in exactly the right places on marked pegboard racks. I hate being so persnickety. I compensate by basking in informality. Our home is the mark of informality. I dress informally and conduct informal church services. I am a perfectionist in creating an aura of informality! If others do not approach their capabilities, that is their privilege. Perhaps they are fearful of their own abilities, or worse yet, perhaps I am the source of their fear in completing a particular task. I would hate to have to satisfy me!

Each of us is struggling for acceptance from people judged to be significant to us. Instead of a freedom in Christ, we exploit a set of self-conceived standards and become annoyed when others select different standards.

In our group life, we are free to experiment with and discover the reality of freedom in Christ. We are free because we know that our criticisms are really about ourselves and can therefore be discussed as a part of a search for desired understanding. When something about a fellow participant becomes a genuine obstruction between us, it needs to be aired. It is not criticism, but a cry for help.

As a child, I was never allowed to go barefooted. For years I have been on my own children to put on shoes whenever I see them barefooted. At a retreat at the Yokefellow Institute in Richmond, Indiana, Craig Peters, the leader at that particular time, had us take off our shoes and socks. I did so, but wondered about such a peculiar request. With Craig's help I discovered all kinds of things about my own need to keep my "ugliness" hidden. We shared a ten-toed fellowship in which we found we could accept one another despite self-judged ugliness of one kind or another. From that point on, if anyone forgot my name he could always point me out as the one going barefooted. A quiet call for help was answered. Now it is totally immaterial to me whether I have shoes on or not. It is a matter of choice, not necessity. There is no self-imposed rule of propriety but a genuine freedom in Christ.

Do you have self-imposed laws that prevent you from doing things that may correspond to what you dislike in others? What does your own list of dislikes tell you about you?

Paraphrase No. 5
(Philippians 3:1–11)

In closing, my Christian brothers, be happy and fulfilled in the service of Jesus Christ. It doesn't bother me to always be telling you the same thing over and over, and it is just what you need.

Look out for the Jews with their stupid ceremonial customs! We are the ones who truly fulfill God's requirement by worshiping him as one who cannot be nailed down to one time or place. We put our trust in what Jesus Christ has done rather than what we can do ourselves.

If anyone has a right to point to his own obedience to ceremonial mumbo jumbo, I do! I was circumcised according to the letter of the law. I can trace my family tree back through the Israelites to Benjamin's tribe. I'm a full-blooded Hebrew. As a Pharisee, I know all about the law. As far as social action is concerned, I led the Jews in trying to kill off the Church. If you can make it by walking the straight and narrow, I've got it made.

But whatever Brownie points I may have been able to accumulate by so-called holiness, I count as zilch! In fact, nothing is worth anything to me in comparison to my relationship with Jesus Christ.

Because of my relationship with him, I have lost a lot, but I consider it all garbage anyway, because, by casting my lot with Christ, I have given up any try at winning Brownie points with God and measure my worth only by what attributes of Christ have rubbed off on me.

I'm putting all my eggs in one basket, and that is the hope that by sharing Christ's way of life, I too will not face extinction at death, but will continue some type of afterlife.

Chief idea to me: Self-worth determined by Christlikeness.
Chief idea to you?

So what?

[6]

Awareness
of
Self

Experiment No. 6

THIS WEEK, think about your own death. What does this assignment do to you in terms of your feelings? For example, do you think such an assignment is morbid or embarrassing? Describe your feelings as you approach the assignment.

What does your death mean to you? What bothers you most about the fact of your own death? Is the certain fact of your death influencing your life in any way now?

Is it possible to make our death as well as our life significant? How would you go about it?

Handle this assignment as three general-area questions. Do not restrict yourself to the questions asked above, but consider the areas they represent. Roughly, these areas are:

1. Your feelings about discussing or thinking about death.
2. What does death really represent to you as a person?
3. What can be done to make death a positive value?

NOTES:

Awareness of Self: Experiment No. 6

During my seminary days, one of my favorite professors would frequently give his critique of student sermons by scolding, "Don't try to scare me by telling me I'm going to die. I already know that!" Unfortunately, not everyone shares his insight in a significant way. Death has become the great American hang-up. In an era of unsurpassed longevity, the threat of death is the most effective means by which to gain attention. The mass media use the fear of death to control or influence our behavior. Anti-cigarette spot announcements are not directed at the life problems of cancer or the survivors of a cancer victim. They are aimed at the smoker's fear of impending death. Skyjackers and political extremists use the threat of death to gain temporary advantages. The problems stemming from environmental pollution were ignored until we were told they would kill us if they continued.

There is little possibility of living a meaningful life until the fact of inevitable death is faced. This is a traumatic psychological confrontation for some, but absolutely essential. At least two reasons come readily to mind.

First, the fear of death can lead to the strangulation of life. Many persons yield to meaningless life styles for no other reason than that they are life-preserving. Such a person may refuse to visit distant friends or go on exciting vacations because of the dangers inherent in traveling. Even local events are avoided because of the crowds attracted and resultant danger of traffic accidents. An airplane flight to the beauties of Switzerland would be absolutely out of the question! One lady I knew had a heart condition and was told by her physician to not climb stairs. She lived across the street from a lovely small park in which she loved to stroll. However, she let the three steps from her porch to the sidewalk hold her a virtual prisoner in her own home for five years. In fear of death she ceased to live.

Children raised in such an atmosphere find themselves subject to the same smothering of life. They are not to climb

69

trees because they might fall. They are not to swim in the ocean because they might drown. They are not to ride bicycles because they might be hit. They are encouraged to avoid certain occupations as they grow up because of the dangers involved. They are not encouraged to embrace life but to preserve it. Many have grown up in this atmosphere. Many continue to perpetuate it.

The second reason is a positive one. Given a certainty of death, a person is free to choose a deliberate life style that counts for something. Consider the person who is advised by a physician that he or she has only a limited and specified time to live. Repeatedly, we have seen persons with terminal illnesses embrace life for the first time. They have had to confront their own finiteness and have discovered the joy of living. Unfortunately, this is usually for a relatively short period of time. By confronting the fact of our own death, we make the first step in discovering a zest for life. We find it possible to embrace a deliberate life style that will reflect our love affair with life. This gives us a new insight into the psychological as well as theological truth of Jesus' injunction that we must lose life to gain it (Mark 8:35).

Within the development of our small groups, we have experienced more divergency of attitude in completing this experiment than perhaps any other. It is imperative that both group and leader listen carefully and avoid any semblance of teaching. Many persons are helped immeasurably by simply verbalizing their fears. It is not necessary for the group or leader to "fix" these fears. The tendency to do so is more likely a measure of one's own insecurity in considering death. Some persons will be openly hostile toward this experiment and resent the question being raised. Many others will reflect a careful working through of the whole problem prior to coming to the group.

By this time, the group should have developed sufficient maturity to preclude anyone's evading the potentials of the experiment by escaping unchallenged into a poor theology gained on grandmother's knee. The tip-off is an unnatural use of "churchy" language not used before and a poetic reference to the illusory nature of death. Death is not an illusion but a fact. The fact of the resurrection does not alter the prior fact of death. Death is the ending point of life-hopes, both for the person who has died and for the survivors who must deal with their own feelings concerning the vestiges of that life. The crucifixion preceded the resurrection. The end of men's life-hopes precedes the beginning of a resurrection-hope in God.

What can be done to make death a positive value? Few persons gain any satisfaction from the bizarre admiration of the undertaker's skill, but they do not know how to be part of a creative alternative. Individual churches frequently provide excellent leadership in this matter, but normally they enter the discussion only after the death has occurred. There is a great need to allow the death event to become a chosen part of the significant witness of a person's life style prior to death.

For many persons, the simple task of preparing a will is a significant first step. A will is a tacit recognition of the inevitability of death. It is unfortunate that many persons feel wills are only for the wealthy. Each state has its own laws concerning the handling of estates, but all appear to favor the wisdom of preparing wills. A properly prepared will reduces both the time and pain required to help the living regain a life orientation. It helps assure that unnecessary additional burdens and worries are not added to the load of grief already assumed. A will not only carries out the desire of the deceased in distributing property, but in protecting the integrity of the family relationship. I was somewhat surprised to discover that in my own state, lacking a will, the estate is divided equally among the surviving spouse and children. This would mean that without a will, my wife,

71

upon my death, would have to pay bills and support the children without adequate resources. Part of our meager estate would simply be held in trust for the children until they come of age. This is contrary to our family life style. We share with one another out of a motivation of love and in response to need. Without a will, the state would offset the integrity of this relationship and provide a mechanical protection for our children, at the expense of the family's immediate welfare.

There has never been greater need and reason to examine our attitudes toward our physical bodies after death than now. Our thoughts will have to be guided by a sound theology concerning the limitation of the containers which have served us so well during the period of our life. The population explosion has generated a parallel land boom. A burial plot is the most expensive real estate we can ever buy. The entire commercial industry built up around the disposal of a no-longer-needed body is unbelievably expensive. At the same time, government welfare programs have assured that almost anyone wishing to be buried can be so honored. These same programs have resulted in a severe side effect. Medical schools can no longer find a desirable number of cadavers for use in training the future savers of life in their chosen profession. At a time when the ability to make life-saving organ transplants is growing rapidly, the availability of such transplants is severely limited.

If one's theology allows, it would appear to be a ripe time for the Christian to act out a witness of the transitory nature of his humanness seen in the light of all that is eternal. Once this decision is confronted and made, it is an easy matter to make arrangements with the medical department of a state university to accomplish your specific wishes. You can will all your vital organs for immediate transplant at the time of death. In a very genuine manner, your death may be a life-giving event for many. By designating that your body may be used for study by medical students, you may well be participating in the extension of life to many other unknowns. Some universities even allow the donor to leave a short personal note to the student who will receive the body for study. Present funeral customs too frequently attempt to deify "that which was." It seems to me the Christian should witness to "that which continues to be," using even the fact of death as an opportunity to serve his fellow-man.

Perhaps the funeral service itself, with its attendant customs, provides the most readily apparent opportunity to provide death with a positive value. The crassness, perhaps even obscenity, of many existing funeral customs has been the subject of many books and does not need repeating here. I will attempt to deal only with the positive potentials.

The barbaric custom of viewing the body at a funeral home should be eliminated. If this serves a legitimate need for others, at least the family should be spared the pain of endless hours of meeting friends under these circumstances in the totally foreign atmosphere of the funeral home. Let the family remain home and meet friends in familiar surroundings if they wish to come. The church community can fulfill the responsibility of meeting with those at the funeral home if this must be continued.

The service, whether it be a funeral service or a memorial service, should be conducted in the church. This is the scene of all our important moments together. There we have shared bread and wine. We have baptized our children or been baptized ourselves in the church. It was the scene of our marriage and the center of our life together as we shared both the good and the bad. What a travesty it would be to turn at the time of our death to the unfamiliar surroundings of a funeral home!

If there is a casket, let it be covered in order that attention not be fixed on the cabinetmaker's art. If there must be flowers, let them be restricted to those which would be in

ME, YOU, AND GOD

good taste during a service of worship. Do you want your
friends to surround you with perhaps a thousand dollars
worth of flowers that will be wilted within a few days, or is
it perhaps more consistent with your sense of values that they
contribute to some work of service among the living that has
your complete endorsement?

Let the service be a balanced recognition of death and life.
It must help your family and friends deal with the fact of
your death and the loneliness they must feel. Let it, however,
give witness to a confidence in the resurrection! The fact of
death and the fact of the resurrection find themselves as
opposite ends of a teeter-totter. When one is down, it is time
to bring it into balance by the force of the other. By the same
token, those most desperately needing such an element of
confidence must be given it by others of the Christian community less personally involved in the pain of their own grief.
The service should be a worship service directed to God, not
a sharing of unmanageable helplessness as men. The con-
gregation should sing hymns together and attempt to minister effectively to the needs of one another. It is truly a time
for proclaiming in the presence of God, "The worst has
happened, but it is not the end."

Perhaps other possibilities will occur to the reader. It is imperative to realize that unless you are willing to confront the
fact of your own death and deal with it positively, your
own death will serve no better purpose than many others you
have seen. You must be the one to openly state that your
death must be different in its significance and to implement
the prior planning necessary to assure that it becomes so.

This does not imply that everyone should sit down and
plan his own funeral, though many persons have done so
meaningfully. It does imply that there are certain minimum
requests that must be stated clearly in advance. In my own
case for instance, I have written a very brief letter of instruc-

tions to my church board. In it, I specify a closing hymn that says what I want persons to remember as they leave the memorial service. Most important of all, as an expression of my understanding of the Christian community, it specifies that no "outside" clergyman is to be brought in to conduct the service. We have shared our lives together. We have ministered to one another throughout life, and I do not want the fact of death to find us unable to continue so to do.

I hope that this discussion gives you a springboard as a point of departure for your own thinking. You will have to discover the answers that are right for you as a uniquely different human being. I can only assure you that *no* answers will be forthcoming as long as you refuse to accept the fact that you were born to die. By hindsight, you know that God was with you at the time of your birth. I am confident that the day will come when, by hindsight, you will know that God was with you at the time of your death.

Paraphrase No. 6
(Philippians 3:12–21)

I don't figure that I already have this resurrection business made by a long shot, but since Christ has put his brand on me I find I am compelled to pattern my life after his, although I'm a long ways from being successful at it.

No, sir, I don't have it made at all, but one thing's for sure—the past is dead and buried. From now on I'm aiming my sights at what I feel God wants me to do with my life. It seems to me that all of us who have gone beyond Christianity as some sort of "spiritual pacifier" have this intent in common. Let's just hang on to our intentions.

I hope you'll follow my lead. There are so many professed

Christians whose lives show they don't understand about the cross or its significance. They see Christianity as a way to the comfortable life and that's all they are concerned with—the here and now.

We aren't really at home in the here and now, though. Our home is in another dimension, and we're waiting for our rescuer, Jesus Christ, to take us from the pain of the here and now to the peace of sharing his resurrection.

Chief idea to me: The past is dead, and the future is no threat, so there is much to accomplish in the present.
Chief idea to you?

So what?

[10]
Awareness
of
Self

Experiment No. 7

TRY TO RECALL and describe your most unique "religious experience." We are using "religious" here in its broadest sense. We are not talking about an experience that was necessarily mystical in nature, but one through which you experienced a confrontation with the source and reason for your own being. If possible, try to recall and relive an experience that had some great effect on you, perhaps changed your entire course of living and changed you. Report on it next week to the group.

NOTES:

Most of us have experienced one or more very special events that have greatly influenced our lives at some point. As the years pass, we hesitate to share such experiences for various reasons. Perhaps someone will laugh. Perhaps it will sound childish or immature. Perhaps it will not even be believed.

Such events are delicate experiences. Almost without exception, they have appealed to us on a feeling level. They do not lend themselves well to a factual, unemotional recounting. They are more to be shared than told. Perhaps the distinction is a fine one, but you may be sure many such experiences of deep significance will remain locked within silent hearts unless your group is sensitive to the difference. The experience of sharing in this experiment is akin to that of sharing a beloved symphony, a cultured rose, or a rare wine. It is not a time to satisfy the intellect, but a time of intense sensitivity to the communication of feelings.

Since we seldom share the experiences that will be prompted by this experiment, they have a tendency to escape from our own conscious memory. We are left with the effects of our special "religious experience" rather than the memory of it. Consequently, we may have developed certain attitudes and feelings with no conscious recollection of their origin. In this final experiment in awareness of self, we will try to recall some such important moment in order better to understand the present person we have become.

This is a deeply emotional experiment for most participants. Words and tears may flow quietly and meaningfully in equal amounts. For some, it may open a forgotten fountain of joy and exuberance. It is an opportunity to accept one another where and as we are.

I would not take anything for some of the experiences I have been privileged to share in our groups. I feel my own life has been blessed with several experiences that were deeply meaningful to me, but they always seem to pale in my own sight as I share the intensely moving feelings of others. I hesitate to even mention them here. It is not the stories in and of themselves that are so impressive, but the feelings that are communicated through them. The stories themselves belong to those who have lived them, and I feel I lack the right to repeat them.

I have listened to both men and women describe their reactions to the wonder of birth. The burliest man and most fearful woman can alike be completely captivated by this supreme miracle of God.

For others, an encounter with a person involved in his own love affair with God was an experience of intense meaning. These were never the self-appointed martyrs, but those who had become self-sacrificing without really being aware of it. One such person was a young woman confined to an iron lung. Her courageous love for life, despite its physical limitations, has been the touchstone by which others have begun to live.

In the Book of Genesis, we are told that God created from chaos. Many of our group members have shared experiences in which God first became real to them as One who broke into their own experience of utter chaos. For some, it was in the midst of death and destruction on a battlefield. For others, it was during the collapse of a family relationship or a lifelong business venture. For still others, it was during the pain of mental or physical incapacity. Attempted suicide, alcoholism, premarital pregnancy, divorce, abandonment—all have been experiences of chaos from which God has woven a positive creation. That which was seen as the end of life became the beginning of a greater life.

With great trepidation, I will share one intensely meaningful experience in my own life. I have seldom shared it and never with anyone with whom I have not developed

80

a rapport of mutual concern and acceptance. Even as I type the words, I fear that a reader will laugh, scoff, or judge it meaningless. Such is the difficulty with which we bring ourselves to share that which may be most meaningful to us.

A few years ago, I was a helicopter pilot stationed in Germany. I had already decided to leave my military career and enter the ministry upon my return from overseas. As a routine part of our flight proficiency, each of us scheduled training flights to unfamiliar destinations for the navigational practice. I decided to make one such training flight to a city near the East German border where a chaplain I greatly respected was stationed. I wanted to talk to him for a few hours and get his recommendations concerning several seminaries I had in mind.

A few days before my planned flight, all our helicopters were grounded for inspection of a mechanical defect experienced on a similar aircraft back in the United States. A defective tail rotor bolt had caused invisible stress forces upon a tail rotor blade, and a helicopter had been completely demolished while sitting on the ground when it lost one of its two tail rotor blades. The loss of one blade causes a severe whip-like motion in which the rear of the aircraft is shaken back and forth like a rat being shaken by a dog. We were told that the helicopter had been destroyed almost instantly and similar model helicopters were grounded world-wide until they had been inspected.

The aircraft I was later to fly was not at our field when the grounding order came but was on a VIP mission at another field. Consequently, other than normal arrangements were made to have it inspected. The resultant inspection may have been made properly or it may not have. I have no way of knowing. At any rate, an inspection was made and the aircraft certified safe to fly.

I flew this particular helicopter on my training flight and

had an uneventful arrival. During my time on the ground at my destination, however, the weather closed in, and I found myself grounded for forty-eight hours.

Those forty-eight hours were the heart of my "religious experience." I was at a point in my Christian pilgrimage where God seemed to be in complete and undeniable control of every little aspect of my life. Even today, I have not been able to retain the full impact of that feeling. For that period of forty-eight hours, nothing happened by chance! Events that would have annoyed me at another time became deeply significant. I called a post taxi to check in at the airfield. It didn't come for an hour, but during that hour I met a man with whom God had intended for me to talk. The waitress in the dining room brought me the wrong order, and as a result I was able to share the love of God with her as she poured out a story of frustration. Each and every moment of those forty-eight hours was crammed with the deliberate presence of God as a living force. I may have trouble explaining the Holy Spirit, but I have no hesitancy in saying that I have met him!

At the end of forty-eight hours, I received weather clearance to leave. The weather was marginal, with low-hanging clouds, but sufficient for helicopters. After a routine preflight of the aircraft, I strapped myself in and started the engine. While it was warming up, I did something I had never done up to that time. I bowed my head and said, "Lord, you have been in charge of everything else the last few days. You can take charge of this flight back home too." It seemed the only natural thing to do and still does. The tower cleared me for take-off, and I started for home. Everything was normal until I had climbed to about five hundred feet three miles from the airfield. Suddenly, there was a sound like a giant spring being wound so tight it broke, and the aircraft pitched up and to the right. I had lost my tail rotor control and knew it immediately. This is one of many anticipated emergencies for which a helicopter pilot is thoroughly trained. It is an especially dangerous situation since without the anti-torque force of the tail rotor, the helicopter may begin spinning in a direction opposite the main rotor blades. I had an instructor's rating in this particular aircraft and was thoroughly proficient in every aspect of handling it. Reacting instantly, I cut power from the engine to stop the spinning tendency, dropped the "collective pitch" control to the bottom, and turned in to the wind. Under these conditions, the aircraft is allowed to drop rapidly in a controlled descent of about 1500 feet per minute until about three feet from the ground. The pitch is then pulled back into the main rotor blades and the helicopter's descent checked and cushioned for the touchdown. Forward speed is maintained somewhat and a ground skid of about thirty feet or more is anticipated. Many things have to be done instantly and correctly. There is no room for error, but even fledgling pilots are trained to react properly. I radioed the tower on my way down that I had lost tail rotor control and they began their crash procedures immediately.

The descent to three feet only took a matter of seconds. The trick in this case is to maintain sufficient airspeed to keep the helicopter "streamlining" in a straight-ahead attitude, but at the same time to maintain the lowest airspeed possible to reduce the ground skid. I have never felt more calm nor had an aircraft respond more perfectly. As I prepared to make the critical correction at three feet altitude I felt like a million dollars. The shock came during those last three feet. I began to apply pitch, but it didn't even seem necessary. I was doing the right things and knew what to do, but they didn't even seem to be necessary. The helicopter settled those last three feet almost completely by itself. I will never forget the feeling or the words I spoke aloud spontaneously, "This is ridiculous!" I settled into a potato field with absolutely no ground skid whatsoever. The skids settled onto the ground gently and didn't scratch so much as an inch of ground.

By the time I shut off the engine and unstrapped myself to get out and check the damage, another helicopter from the airfield was approaching. The other pilot and I shared the inspection in amazement. The entire tail rotor assembly and a part of the tail boom were missing!

I am a heavy man. Without the weight of these parts at the extreme tail-end of the aircraft to counteract my own weight in the cockpit, the helicopter should have dropped nose first completely out of balance. It is like having someone jump off the other end of a teeter-totter. During the next few hours, we found the missing pieces of the helicopter in a densely wooded area. It quickly became apparent that a disaster should have occurred, but had not.

One tail rotor blade had broken off in flight, just like the one that had previously destroyed a similar helicopter sitting on the ground. Apparently, the first violent reaction from the missing blade was sufficient to break off the rest of the tail section instantly. If that had not happened, I would not have been in one piece by the time I hit the ground. On the other hand, this loss of weight should have thrown me out of balance and sent me down out of control.

I am sure that God did not change any of the natural laws of his universe for my benefit. I think a computer, if fed all the appropriate data, could tell me why I am still alive. A multitude of factors had to dovetail perfectly at precisely the right moment, and they did. The symbol of the Holy Spirit is the dove, and I have no doubt whatsoever that he was totally responsible for this critical dovetailing operation.

The effect on other pilots was interesting, even hilarious by hindsight. I became a marked man. They would look at the helicopter, look at me, and walk off shaking their heads. At the club, pilots would walk up to me and ask, "Are you the guy who landed that helicopter without the tail?" and again shake their heads and walk off. When pilots of my own unit came to pick me up, they repeated the same now-familiar pattern. In the sight of the event, words were useless. I had taken a bit of a ribbing from some of my fellow officers for submitting my resignation from the regular Army to enter seminary. Now they seemed to understand. Our group commander even began to ask me to open staff meetings with prayer. That in itself would have been a sufficient miracle for one lifetime.

As the experience has become a part of an almost forgotten past life history, it has found its own place in my understanding of God. During my seminary days that followed the event, I studied the phrase "Be still, and know that I am God" (Psalm 46:10). As a result of this study, I was confronted by the Hebrew word *raphah*, translated as "still." It does not mean to be still in the sense of silence, but in the sense of relaxing a tight grasp or tenacious activity. It could be more precisely translated, "Relax, and know that I am God." I had done precisely that for one short flight. If I had not, I would not be here today. My experience made that *living* Scripture for me!

Paraphrase No. 7
(Philippians 4:1–23)

My dearest friends, be solid Christians. I ask Mert and Gert to quit arguing. You are my partners as Christians. These women have also been, so I hope you will help them now.
Let your relationship with Christ fill you with happiness. Become known for your patience. Christ is with us. Don't

give in to worries, but let him carry the load for you. Then you will know the reality of peace by letting him control your heart and mind.

In closing, my brothers, keep your minds on the highest possible ideals. Do what you have been taught as Christians, and you will find peace.

I am very happy that your concern for me has taken the form of action. Not that I have it so rough—I've learned to be satisfied with whatever life brings me. I've had my ups and downs and learned to live with both by relying on Christ rather than my own strength.

Still, I appreciate the way you have shared the problems of my imprisonment. You were the only ones to share both the good and the bad when I left Macedonia. The same goes for Thessalonica.

It's not that I look forward to what you share with me. It's the effect it has on you that is important.

I couldn't ask for more. You have satisfied all my needs with the gifts sent by Epy; gifts offered to God's service in this way. Have no fear—God will supply all your needs if you ever are in this position. He's the greatest.

Tell all the gang hello for me. All the Christians here send their best, especially those working for Caesar. May the joy of Christ's presence be with you.

PAUL

Chief idea to me: Pass it on to others who need you now.
Chief idea to you?

So what?

[11]

A
Night
Off

IF YOU HAVE BEEN carrying out your experiments faithfully,
you will be ready for a holiday. The series of experiments
on awareness of self, although exciting, can be a genuine
drain on the emotions. We have found a night of low-key
relaxation to be especially helpful in making the bridge to
the ensuing experiments on awareness of others. It is a
night with a purpose. With effective planning, it is a valuable terminating point for one group of experiments and
a helpful starting point for the next.

I suggest you plan a potluck dinner for your group. Let
everyone bring a favorite dish and simply share the joy of
one another's presence. It is helpful if the dinner can be
planned for someone's home, perhaps the leader's. Your
church may have a more suitable place from the standpoint of convenience and room, but your homes will have
a special significance for you by now. Don't worry about a
dining table or impressive setting. Simply put the food out
where everyone may help himself, fill his paper plate, and
sit around the living room floor and have fun!

While everyone is munching on dessert, bring up the
question of the Scripture the group wishes to study during
the rest of your time together. This should be selected by
group consensus. It is well to steer clear of books that may

give someone an opportunity to become a "teacher." If a guideline is helpful, I would recommend the Book of Mark. Mark presents the simplest and most direct narrative of the facts of the life of Christ. Its length is ideal for the study of a chapter a week for the remaining period still before the group. Paraphrases are no longer desirable.

We have found it helpful to promote a rule against the use of biblical commentaries during this period of study. A certain amount of swapping of ignorance is preferable to the development of a small group of experts who threaten everyone else by seeming to know it all. If a question comes up that points to the need of a commentary, someone may be designated by the group to research the question during the ensuing week, with instructions to report findings back to the group. If you are a clergyman group leader, this experience can be a genuine challenge to you as a human being. It will perhaps be difficult for you to refuse to speak from a position of assumed authority. The growth benefits to the rest of the group are incomparable, and your own growth in humility and sensitivity may be a most valuable bonus result.

This would be an appropriate time to question the advisability of abolishing the group leader's role. After experimentation in both approaches, I heartily recommend that the group consciously take over its own leadership. The simplest and most effective means is to agree that the host couple will lead both the Bible study and experiment discussion each week from this point on. This may be a scary prospect for some persons, but it is a wonderful thing to watch their confidence grow as they discover their efforts are being affirmed by honest and loving group members. Perhaps the bigger problem is that of a clergy leader who doesn't really believe in the "priesthood of all believers" when it comes to leadership of a fellowship seeking to be

A Night Off

Christian. Put a pillow at the foot of your pedestal. It is high time you were knocked off!

Now that you are ready for after-dinner coffee, introduce a purposive game. The group leader should prepare for this game in advance by bringing two large pipe cleaners of contrasting color for each person in the group. These can be obtained from any craft shop. After the pipe cleaners have been distributed, give the following instruction:

Construct something from your two pipe cleaners that represents the way you see yourself in relationship with other people.

Let everyone work without further guidance until all have finished. Then go around the circle and let each person in turn show his creation without commenting upon it. Ask everyone else in the group to tell what he thinks he sees. Emphasize that you are talking about the depiction and not the person. Don't restrict this feedback to any order. Let each person interject whatever he wants to when he wants to. After the discussion begins to die down, ask the person who made it to explain his intentions to the rest of the group. Proceed to the next person and so on around the rest of the group.

It is tremendously tempting to share with you the results of this experiment as we have observed them in our groups, but this would tend to stifle your own creativity in discovering the possible meaning for which you will be searching. It is a game with unlimited potential, and it is up to your group to discover significant insights for itself. Along with other more obvious insights, it might be of interest to you to consider the manner in which the contrasting colors are used. Does one have an advantage over the other? If someone shows his creation by throwing it out on the floor rather than holding it, the reasons for such action might profitably be dug into by the group.

After this game has been concluded, it would be appropriate for the leader to make whatever observations might help tie your discoveries together. In addition to any special discoveries you may have made, I would suggest you consider at least the following two points:

1. *Everyone started with identical materials—two pipe cleaners.* Straighten out a set to emphasize the point that we all started at the same place. Our representation of ourself in relationship with others was whatever we chose to make it. By the same token, our actual relationship with others is of our own choosing. It will become whatever we fashion. During the next seven weeks, we are going to be looking at those relationships closely. Our purpose is to give us information upon which we may act as we fashion our own chosen fabric of relationships.

2. *They were only pipe cleaners.* Relationships are composed of individual human beings who are after all only human beings. Many of us fear to enter significant relationships because of a feeling of inferiority to others. The more we desire the relationship, the more likely we are to feel the self-imposed judgment of inferiority. It is an old saw, but nevertheless a true one—the men we respect or fear the most put on their trousers one leg at a time—just like us. Our starting point in the awareness of others proceeds from the discovery of the humanness of others. It will be difficult to set ourselves aside for the next few weeks, but that is our purpose. We hope to discover objectively the human beings who share this world and life with us.

One final activity remains to polish off a delightful evening. Get in touch with one another as members of the group. Go around the horn again and let each person speak in turn.

Where are you as a member of this group? What expec-

tations did you bring with you and how do you feel about yourself and the group?

This is a time of inestimable value together. Some persons will talk about themselves. Others will point out discoveries about their relationship with others in the group. You may be sure that it will be an honest and meaningful exchange of human beings enjoying the freedom of being human. Listen carefully to each person and seek to accept the feelings that are being offered as well as the words. Your discussion together may lead to altering certain facets of your group life, thus enriching the nature of your own unique group. You are beginning to discover and live out that exciting life style we call "Christian community."

[12]
Awareness
of
Others

Experiment No. 1

THIS IS AN INITIAL experiment in awareness of another
person. It will probably show us how difficult it is to really
care enough to become deeply aware of another, even one
close to us.

This week, discover from your spouse what his or her chief
aim is during the current year. Don't guess, and don't work
from past experience. This will be an exercise in listening
and understanding.

For those without mates in our group, choose some person
you know rather well and try to discover the same thing.

NOTES:

The comments I may make on each experiment concerning awareness of others must of necessity be rather limited. One of the more valuable lessons to be learned as we become aware of others is that each and every individual is a distinctive human being. It is in the discovery of the uniqueness of each person that we begin to grow as Christians and to share in the excitement of a Creator's purpose. Individuals cannot be categorized.

This may appear to be at cross-purposes with our discoveries as we became more aware of ourselves. One of our early discoveries, and a comforting one, was that we are all basically very much alike. This is a statement of fact—when our focus of attention is on our basic nature. Perhaps it would be more to the point to say that we are quite similar in the way we *feel* about ourselves. All of us are a bit insecure. All of us need to be loved and to develop the capacity to love. All of us need to be affirmed by those significant in our lives. We are alike at the gut level.

Our awareness of others is normally experienced on a different level. At a recent conference, I was greatly helped in understanding both myself and others through a diagrammatic depiction of man's make-up. I have no idea from what source this depiction was drawn, but it speaks accurately to my experience as a human being. This diagram indicates that there is a part of every person that consists of what he knows or believes to be true. This is the intellectual part of him that reads, thinks, and reasons. There is another part of him that feels. This is the emotional part of him that responds in joy, sorrow, or boredom. There is a third part of each man that acts out. He does something. That something may be based either on his intellect or his feelings.

The mark of a healthy person is the degree to which each of these three factors exist in a balanced and appropriate relationship with each other. Mental institutions are full of troubled people suffering from a severe impairment of this

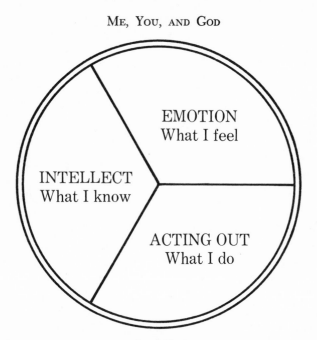

balance. One patient sits huddled in a corner, unable to appropriately act out either his beliefs or his feelings. Another weeps bitterly for hours, acting out feelings that have lost touch with intellectual reason. Yet another is certain there is a plot against his life. His feelings and acting out are consistent with this knowledge that exists in an estrangement with reality. Their hope is through the restoration of that part of them which seems to be missing; that which leaves them lacking essential human balance.

The streets are full of persons existing in varying and changing degrees of appropriate balance and interaction with themselves. Our main contact with them is at the level of their acting out. If we lump into the same category all persons who are acting out similarly, we dehumanize them and cease in that moment to be aware of them as unique persons. We in turn react to them in inappropriate ways. Our lack of understanding returns to affect us, and we too are out of balance.

Typically, we act out our feelings. Curiosity, exercised through our intellect, would probably lead us to a more balanced and more appropriate acting out. We have been conditioned by a lifetime of experience to *react* to others. In other words, we act in response to our feelings about their acts. Our hope, as Christians, is to be able deliberately and appropriately to *act* toward people, rather than *react*.

Let us look at a hypothetical example. A man comes home from a frustrating day's work to his wife, who has also had a trying day. "How're things?" he asks, as he sits down and reaches for the evening paper. "Okay, I guess," she responds, pulling the meat loaf from the oven. Both are tired and both need the affirmation of one another's love. Neither have acted out their feelings appropriately. The wife tries to get her husband's attention by acting out her feelings even more inappropriately. She bangs the dishes on the table and almost throws the silverware. Her husband reacts mentally by guessing that his wife is angry at him for something. She is just one more on his list for the day. He is sure everyone at the office is angry at him too, so he feels hurt, but to avoid further hurt he ignores her. After a few further emotion-escalating acts along the same lines, the wife finally flees to the bedroom and slams the door. Her husband, feeling like a whipped dog, puts on his coat and heads for the nearest bar, muttering, "Women are all the same!"

A slammed door is nothing more than a rapidly closed door. It may be a request for love, a notice that you are about to be shot, or the result of an accidental gust of wind. Any act based upon a slammed door is a *reaction*, not an *action*. The wise man will find out the meaning of the slammed door before he chooses his action. He will act appropriately. He will begin to discover the joy of living as a man rather than a two-legged Ping-Pong ball.

Expect a shocked reaction from your husband or wife as you begin to carry out this experiment. He or she will be suspicious at first. "Why after fifteen years the sudden interest?" Persist, and your mate will be flattered. Really care about what is being said, and he or she will be elated. You may discover your mate is not only unique but pretty wonderful.

[13]
Awareness
of
Others

Experiment No. 2

THIS WEEK, choose one person outside your family to try to be especially aware of. What makes him act the way he does? Get to know that person better if possible. You may want to choose a person whom you have found particularly difficult to get along with or one who puzzles or troubles you. Report on the results of your study of that person. What did you discover about him that you had not noticed before? Why does he act the way he does?

NOTES:

There is an old Indian saying that you do not know a man until you have walked in his moccasins for two miles. This experiment is not intended to be analytical. It is an attempt to stand in someone else's moccasins—to see the world as he sees it.

You may have some reservations about getting behind the veneer of another person's acting out. There is no other way to become aware of the uniqueness of that person. There is no possible manner in which you may act appropriately toward that person until you gain additional insight. There is no reason to fear being judged "nosey" unless you have already determined the manner in which you are going to act toward that person. If you are able to be honestly interested, your interest will be welcomed. If a newspaper writer were to sit at a lunch counter with you and remark, "You're an interesting person. I would like to get to know more about you," you would be more than willing to see that he had the chance. If, on the other hand, the same writer was to say, "I'm going to do an article on how obnoxious you are. Give me some facts about your life," you would leave in a hurry, probably having clobbered the man first.

Several months ago I was talking to a troubled young woman. Despite intense efforts at communication, we just weren't able to find an effective common ground from which to work. Finally, she blurted out, "You just don't understand my world."

"I would like to," I replied. "How about inviting me into it?"

"Okay," she responded, "how about going to see it right now?"

This caught me a little off guard. By my ground rules, I assumed we would see her world through words. On a sudden impulse, I canceled my other appointments and agreed to go with her.

We went to a tiny house in the country where she shared

her home with a young couple and their baby. They had experienced some rough times and could not afford a place of their own. After meeting them, we went outside, and I watched as she selected two hunting dogs from a pen of several that were clamoring for attention. She led them a short distance until they picked up the scent of something, perhaps a passing rabbit. Then, as they yelped with excitement, she released them to seek out their quarry, and we followed them as best we could from their sound. We spent a couple of hours walking through the woods, following winding paths, now and then stopping to look at the tracks of a deer or some other creature of the woods. We stepped in mud and caught our clothes on briars as we passed. It was a world with its own language. It lacked words and people, but it communicated in its own way.

We began to talk again about the same problem we had been discussing in my study. This time we spoke in the language of her world. We talked about winding paths and obstacles that tore at us. We talked about the choice of taking different paths, and whether it was necessary to go all the way back to the house to start over or whether perhaps we could just strike across country from where we stood. We talked about the time we would waste in trying to retrace our route and the relative problem of the mud and thorns we would pick up by seeking a more direct way. I don't remember that any great decisions were made. I do remember the thrill of walking in another's moccasins. I also remember the thrill of a Holy Presence not attributable to either of the faltering human beings who shared that walk.

Risk getting to know others. They will be a little suspicious at first. Not many persons really appear to care. Be consistent in showing that you do care and you will be amazed at the results. Not only will you begin to feel different about others, but you will begin to feel vastly different about yourself. You will also begin to feel different about One who came himself to walk in man's moccasins. He too assumed a great risk. Men were suspicious of him, but he continued to live out his concern consistently. He amazed those with whom he walked. He continues to amaze us.

Some time ago I heard of a minister who resigned his traditional church-centered type of ministry and bought a restaurant. He caters particularly to teenagers. As a group, they are disdained by most restaurant owners. They buy little, linger long, and make lots of noise. This man is unique in that he recognizes each of his customers as individual human beings who just happen to be under twenty-one. Each customer has a face and a name. The owner goes further than this, however. Each customer has an opinion, and it will be listened to and valued. The owner keeps a clipboard behind the counter and, during the lull between orders, reaches for it and approaches one of his young customers. He asks a pertinent question about one of the significant problems of our world, and as his customer responds, he carefully notes what is said. Needless to say, he is loved by his customers. He also loves them. He had to start someplace. I cannot believe he was born with any head start. Once, he had to decide to take the risk. So do we.

[14]

Awareness
of
Others

Experiment No. 3

CAN YOU STIMULATE apparently spontaneous change in the attitude of others? This week, go out of your way to be especially friendly and courteous to all whom you meet—the supermarket check-out girl, the man who works next to you, the post office clerk, etc. Be especially considerate to those who are most gruff toward you and others. Show an interest in these persons. Find out something about them in the moments you are together. See if the way you act toward others will make them act differently. Record your experiences in a daily log and report them to the group.

NOTES:

Awareness of Others: Experiment No. 3

Many of our relationships are casual ones of short duration. It is disturbing to note the prolonged negative influence some of these brief encounters wield. A curt hairdresser may ruin the entire date for which a young lady is preparing. A man's attitude toward a particular product or company may be determined by the mood of a salesman who has just had a fight with his wife. A taxi driver's impatience and sharpness may cause an interpreter for the United Nations to begin the day's work in a bitter mood. A caustic comment by that same interpreter may engender a feeling of annoyance in a frustrated delegate. Is it too great a stretch of imagination to believe that the entire destiny of a nation might be affected as that delegate vents his annoyance in an unguarded moment of spontaneous outburst? When we know one of the world's most influential leaders removed his shoe and pounded it upon the table in anger during a meeting of the United Nations, nothing is beyond the realm of the possible.

Where does this leave us as persons seeking a new life style? Are we the helpless victims of brief, but adverse, encounters? You will accept only the answer your experience tells you is true. The purpose of this experiment is to assure that such a determination is made on the basis of fact, not guess. When your waitress practically sneers at you, ask, "Having a rough evening?" Mean it when you ask, and see what happens. When the service manager assures you for the fourth time in four hours that your car will be ready in an hour, ask him about the problems he has in coordinating the work of so many mechanics. Inquire into the frustrations he has in dealing with customers who are always hostile. Try to understand the man in a good-natured brief encounter and see if his manner toward you changes.

This experiment can be a life-changing one for you. Recall it several times a day and conduct the experiment as frequently as possible. Keep a careful log of each encounter so that you can recall them later in a systematic way. I believe you will be impressed not only by the immediate change in relationships noted, but by the positive warm feelings stirred up when you later recollect each incident. You will undoubtedly experience some encounters you are unable to change. As you recall such an incident by the use of your log, I wonder if you will feel a resurge of annoyance or will experience a burst of laughter. I predict you are in for some pleasant surprises!

[15]

Awareness
of
Others

Experiment No. 4

NONE OF US are self-made persons. All around us, people and forces are influencing us—pressuring us, causing us to change our ways, to buy things, to react, to be angry, to be happy.

The problem is that although many kinds of forces and people are always affecting us, we are not always aware what these forces are and to what extent they are causing us to change.

This week's assignment is to be especially aware of advertisements, propaganda, other people, or what have you, in an effort to determine what forces and people are shaping your life and your decisions for the good and for the bad.

Make a written list of as many of these forces and people as you can identify as influencing your way of life. Bring the list with you to be discussed at the next meeting. Each day, read over this sheet as a reminder of the assignment.

NOTES:

This experiment will unfold in two stages. The importance of the first will be obscured until validated by the second. The first stage is simply to list as many of the forces asked for as possible. Try to categorize them in some way for convenience in referring to them later.

Now we will consider the second stage. This will take place at the meeting of your small group. Listen carefully as each person shares his list. Keep notes on each person, and try to capture, in capsule form, the essence of each person's list. Don't get lost in the multiplicity of forces. Try to find logical categories within which the forces would fall. Compare your notes with what you have come to know of each person. Is there a correlation between the nature of the person and the forces *he chooses to allow* to influence him strongly? The outside forces exerting pressure on us are essentially the same for all. If we choose, we can make positive changes by recognizing the power some wield and refusing to allow them to exert further influence, at the same time choosing to make others a more substantial part of our experience.

One attractive young woman in one of our groups listed forces that enforced group standards. Each in some way delineated some aspect of expected behavior. This young lady walks on eggshells in her relationships. She is always afraid of doing something someone will think is "wrong."

A man listed forces that cause him to react contrariwise. He lives in constant conflict with himself and his wife. Tell him that it is Monday, and he feels compelled to argue that it is Tuesday.

Another man described forces that put him under constant pressure. He experiences continual problems with family and associates because he is unable to establish his own priorities and act upon them. Without pressure, he will never act.

Two men in the same group described influences that

111

were precise opposites. One man listed many forces, all of which had a strong emotional content. The other man listed forces with nonemotional natures. The first man lives from one crisis to another. The latter would not get unduly excited if his trousers were on fire.

Try to assess the persons in your group in the same manner. See if you can establish a clear connection between the nature of people and the forces they permit to influence them.

Once you have a firm grasp on this concept, return to the first stage of the experiment. Look at your own list again. What does it tell you about you? What positive forces could you *deliberately choose* to allow to exert an influence upon you?

Let us see if we can illustrate this point in an admittedly crude way. Let us return to some of the individuals discussed above and select artificial forces for them. We will have to speculate as to whether or not desirable changes would result.

First, the lady of the eggshell world. Let us choose for her all the forces we can imagine that would pressure her to be a nonconformist. Buy a group of biographical books for her about some of the world's greatest nonconformists. Jesus would have to be included. Encourage her to attend controversial movies and stage productions. Perhaps she would even want to participate in amateur dramatic groups where she could play far-out roles. As long as speculating costs nothing, let us move her to an apartment house and encourage her to select an interior decorator with tastes quite opposite her own. Let her develop hobbies and recreational pursuits that are unique. Perhaps she would like to shrink orangutan heads and drive formula racing cars.

We have not done this gal any great favors. We have substituted one set of problems for a different set. We have accomplished one thing, however. We have released her

112

from entrapment. If she could actually try living under the conditions we suggested, she might hate them all. It is to be hoped, however, that she would be able to return to a life style of her own choice, not one that reflects what is expected of her.

Our contrary man desires the benefits of an education he will probably never achieve, at least formally. He has felt inferior for a lifetime, but he is not. He only acts as if it were true. Let him continue to exist within the love of a patient small group who will keep accepting him rather than arguing with him. If it is really important to him, let him subscribe to one of the new cassette tape services that send periodic digests from wide readings to subscribers. He doesn't need factual information, but if he feels it is important, let him have it. Let him know more about more things than anyone else in the group. Maybe it will facilitate the discovery that everyone, including his wife, wants *him*, not his infallible brain.

The man who feels he lives under constant pressure needs only a few moments a day to himself. Let his wife give them to him without making him feel guilty for taking them. Let him enjoy the quiet of a lonely walk, the soul-stirring beauty of a symphony on record, or even the indulgence of a favorite television program alone. Give him the gift of at least thirty totally pressure-free minutes each day.

It should be obvious that each of these suggestions is hopelessly guilty of oversimplification. It will require a long hammering-out process to change our attitudes significantly. There is a starting place, though. We must find the courage to deal with our environment, rather than abdicate to its supremacy. We are not captives. We live as free men in Christ!

[16]

Awareness
of
Others

Experiment No. 5

SCHEDULE AND CONDUCT an interview with a person you admire who is neither a relative nor a member of your small group. Find out in your interview the things this person is most optimistic about; the things he or she feels good about or has hopes for. Find out what it is that keeps this person going—in other words, the substance of his faith.

Compare your findings with your own view of the future as seen from the present and with your own feelings of optimism about the future.

Come prepared next week to share the discoveries arising from this interview.

NOTES:

In conducting an interview such as this, it is important that we not prepare ourselves to hear certain anticipated things. Our ears have a way of reacting to the programing of our minds. We can set up "filters" that permit the passage of only those things we expect to hear. We are striving to be *aware* of another person, not to judge him. We do not want to assess the person's remarks in the light of our own beliefs, but to discover a person—thereby calling into question our own attitudes.

Which comes first, the chicken or the egg? The life we experience causes us to develop a certain attitude toward life. On the other hand, an embraced attitude toward life can lead us to the experience of a different kind of life. This experiment aims at getting the tail out of the dog's mouth long enough to stop the circular chase.

You have deliberately chosen a person you admire. At the least, this means that you have found something attractive about this person's life style. Your purpose is to now find the corresponding attitudes that complement that life style. If you are reading this book without actually conducting the experiments, you stand in danger of working by guess at this point. You will either fantasize a set of attitudes that satisfy your assumptions about a person or you will select a person who satisfies your assumptions about his attitudes. Either way you lose.

This experiment should be conducted in such a totally objective way that you are willing to risk the possibility of no longer admiring the person you thought you admired. I have never experienced this nor known it to happen. Nevertheless, this is the mental attitude of scientific objectivity that should accompany the interview. Don't look for a person who will tell you what you want to hear. Discover the attitudes that honestly accompany the personhood of this person you admire. If he is an atheist or gets his kicks from eating chocolate-covered ants, so be it. The God we seek will reveal himself in people in his own chosen ways. Don't try to coerce him into a preconceived mold.

Learn from a person you admire. Get the facts as that person knows them. Then, and only then, analyze and weigh those facts remembering that this person is living out some quality of life that you find attractive. You are not the same persons. The attitudes you discover cannot cause you to live a corresponding life style. They can and will be elements of discovered information upon which to base your own chosen life style. They are not fences but signposts. As you seek the direction leading to the future of your own life, take your bearings from as many appropriate signposts as you can discover along the way.

A chosen attitude will bring about change. One of the most exciting individuals I know is a young lady who used to be a mouse before being kissed by the handsome prince— in this case, the Prince of Peace. She was crippled by feelings of inferiority, sure she was unloved and unlovable, and so on. Her husband was unexpectedly sent overseas under circumstances that prevented her accompanying him. She was left at the mercy of all those people whom she was certain could not possibly find her worthy of loving. One day she discovered that Christ loved her exactly as she was. I am not even sure how it happened. She had been "taught" that as fact before. It had never meant too much. Suddenly, she discovered it as fact for herself, and a whole community has been learning from her ever since. This one attitude became a dynamo with endless power. I still don't understand it all. The same attitude affects my life, but not to the extent it does hers. Every time this experiment is assigned to one of the small groups in our church, her phone rings and someone wants to interview her. Some leave bewildered. Some leave with a new attitude—and a changed life.

[17]
Awareness
of
Others

Experiment No. 6

WE DEPEND ON many other people all the time. This week, and from now on, be especially aware of the many things that are done for you by others. But don't stop there! Take positive action. Begin writing thank-you notes—just short ones to people who have been important to you. Search for people to whom you are grateful. It will take much work at first, for we all take a great deal for granted.

The value of this experiment lies in the pre-planning—in looking for points of good in others from day to day. If the thank-you notes are merely used as an afterthought, they have no value other than common courtesy.

Write at least one note each day during the coming week. Don't discriminate. The good may come from someone important in your daily life or from someone you never noticed before.

NOTES:

Because of his position, every pastor receives encouraging notes from sincere parishioners from time to time. Most are a variation of the "that-was-a-good-sermon" compliment. They are appreciated, but I have always suspected most were the results of sensitive people exercising a thoughtful courtesy. I will never forget the thrill of receiving a different kind of note. It said simply, "Thank you for being you." It so happened that it came to me in the mail at a time when I was depressed for some reason. What a lift that note gave! Here was a person appreciating me as a human being, rather than commenting on the value of my function. That person strongly influenced not only that particular day, but my entire attitude about the future. It made me sensitive in a fresh way to the many wonderful people all around me who felt they were living alone in a threatening world. I began writing notes too. Short, to the point, honest. The feedback from some of those notes brought tears to my eyes. God was very obviously at work. The incredible sense of appropriate timing defied any other explanation.

This is a life-changing mission anyone can share. If a note is simply common courtesy, it points back to us and has little impact. If it comes from an open heart, it points to God without even mentioning his name. You will be convinced of the truth of this only by your own experimentation. Write notes that are honest attempts at expressing your feelings, and lives will be changed. If you are doubly fortunate, a few persons will let you know just how much their lives were changed. The impact of your own words could not produce such a change by themselves. The change points to God's involvement through a pyramiding effect—your honesty, another's need, and the multiplying concern of God.

Do not be a name dropper. We have been taught some pretty bad theology concerning "witnessing" along the way. We feel we have "witnessed" only if we have slipped God's name, or a variation on the theme, into the conversation.

Notes say, "God cares for all his children." "May the peace of God enter your heart." "God loves you." Many are dutifully signed, "In Christ." If we communicate our own sincere love, the ground is prepared for the realization and growth in awareness of God's love. If we dodge our own human involvement, the person to whom we speak has no bridge over which the love of God can come. The seed of love is not thus planted, but only religious words. Let us not be persuaded into going through life as word planters. God is not a holy dictionary. He is a living intervener in the life history of man.

You will find what you look for in people. Look for evil, and you will be overwhelmed by the evil found all around you. Look for good, and you will be overwhelmed by the good you find. Appeal to that good, and it will grow. Ignore it, and it may eventually wither for lack of cultivation. The Bible is realistic and quite specific in pointing out that the life experience is always a simultaneous intermixed growth of good and bad (Matt. 13:24-30). Being a destroyer of the bad is discouraged and pointed out as the prerogative of God alone. Man is to be the cultivator and encourager of good. We are charged with the task of affecting the critical balance. This experiment is an exciting participation with God. At first you may think you are doing something by yourself. Stick with it, and you will eventually begin to hear some feedback that will convince you of your partnership with God.

[18]

Awareness
of
Others

Experiment No. 7

THIS IS THE final experiment in awareness of others. In the previous series of experiments, you developed an awareness of yourself. Now, let's combine the two:

"We do not see things as they are, but as we are." As you try to increase your sensitivity toward others, notice how your view of them is related to your mood of the moment, and/or your general outlook on life.

Next week, keep this principle in the center of all your conscious attitudes towards people. Put it into practice for just one week and see what happens to you and the way you see all things. This has to be a daily exercise. Don't wait until the day before our next meeting!

NOTES:

Every winter, my furnace filters have to be changed. Periodically, I have to inspect them and be sure they are in condition to function properly. This experiment involves the inspection of our *human* filters.

The claim to total objectivity in the awareness of another person is a myth! Even a photograph is a depiction of what is seen from only a certain chosen angle. Each of us has a built-in set of filters through which the awareness of experiences must pass. We are quickly aware of those experiences passing through to us easily. We need to become aware also of the residues of valid experience building up on the other side of our filters.

A human being, especially one attempting to be a Christian, should always be suspicious of his conclusions. This does not mean that we do not form strong impressions. We do. We also establish conclusions upon which to base our actions. All these, however, must be tentative. They are accepted as being useful until new impressions help us construct more appropriate conclusions. We always "see through a glass, darkly" (1 Cor. 13:12, KJV).

There is no group as arrogant in its claims to having the ultimate truth as one formed on the basis of religion. Go to a bar, and you may find people willing to make an honest search for the truth about God or any other subject. Go to a church, and you may well find yourself ostracized if you do not conform to its members' beliefs on baptism, salvation, the "second blessing," or a host of other doctrinal beliefs that will be argued as if with ultimate authority at the dropping of a hat. Man is stuffed to the ears with pride. He has to know all; then on the basis of his knowledge he begins "playing God" with people. We can know only as much as God has revealed to us at any given time in history! Let us be satisfied with that and in humble ignorance wait for further revelation.

We cannot develop one attitude for our religious life as

it is lived through the formalities of established religious practices and another attitude for use in everyday life. Christ cannot be cut apart along the dotted line and divided into a secular world existing apart from a sacred one. There is one Christ. He is the Christ of all of life. Our attitudes and our filters exist in the validity of all of life. If we can but examine the filters that influence our awareness of other human beings, we will discover something valid to be applied to our total life experience.

Let me give a simple example to illustrate this point. I am sure each and every one of us at some time has been in a great hurry and found himself forced to wait in a line. Assume this particular instance in a supermarket check-out line. We frown, we shift weight from one foot to the other nervously, we sigh, we mutter, we may even make sarcastic comments to anyone who will listen. After what seems an eternity, we finally get to the car. We have worked ourselves into a fit of short temper. We yell at the kids without reason. We finally get all the sacks in the trunk and slam the lid with great zest. Muttering at any traffic slowing our departure from the parking lot, we start for whatever destination was so pressing. Eventually, we cool off a bit and complain, "That woman was the slowest check-out girl I have even seen!" Not so; back up a minute. It is quite probable that she was neither more nor less efficient than at any other time. We are filtering our observation of her through the filter of our own impatience, caused by being in an unusual hurry. Every experience that does not elude that filter becomes an obstacle. Here is an important discovery about ourselves. By generalizing, we might conclude that *whenever we get in a hurry, our perceptions of reality become grossly distorted.*

We have now discovered something valid about our filtering mechanisms. Apply this principle to prayer life. If prayer is not immediately effective within what we feel is an adequate time, our conclusions about the validity of prayer

126

will reflect an error induced by our impatience. Apply this principle to the experience of religious conversion. If a person does not respond within a "reasonable" time to a deliberate attempt at evangelism, we may become pessimistic about the person's future. Apply this principle to the life of the church. If our particular church does not appear to be following some sort of invisible timetable we have for it, we may be led to make erroneous conclusions about its state of health. Apply this principle to a business situation. If an executive fails to gain an important contract by the established suspense date, the executive may well be judged incompetent. Recognize the influence the time factor is imposing on each of these situations, and we stand a much better chance of making a more appropriate and more effective conclusion.

Each of us has to do his own homework on his distinctive set of filters. We could easily establish a list that would cover all of us to some extent. The list would necessarily be generalized, just as is the example above on impatience. Each of us will profit to a far greater degree by discovering specific filters that apply in a unique way and to a determined degree.

Become extremely sensitive to the operation of such specific elements in your own life day by day for one week. Once discovered and deliberately acted upon, they will move to the conscious part of your reasoning methods. You will become a more adequate human being. That is a big step toward becoming a more effective Christian. It is also a prerequisite for participating honestly in the next set of experiments, those aimed at developing an awareness of God.

[19]
Awareness
of
God

Experiment No. 1

ONE MOMENT OF vulnerability in an experimental relationship with God is more valuable than a million words written about the discoveries of others. For that reason, the experiments in this section will be presented without comment of any kind. Experiment completely and honestly. Develop your own conclusions!

During this series of experiments, we commit ourselves to the discipline of daily Bible study. Study is not really a good description of the purpose, however. Perhaps we should say "Bible exposure." Each of us is to select a specific time of the day, and during that time read as short or as long a passage from the Bible as we desire. Here are the rules:

1. Read "thinking positively." Read convinced that God is going to communicate something to you that you had never before seen in just that way—something important to your daily life.

2. When you have completed your selected passage, write the date at the bottom of the passage.

3. Keep a dated notebook in which you jot down the outline of new or inspiring thoughts that have come to you during your time of reading.

4. For this series of experiments, select for your reading Paul's letter to the rather new Christians in Corinth that we know as 1 Corinthians.

5. No commentaries please. This is not an exercise in seeing what you can dig out, but one in which you are sensitive to what God chooses to reveal.

Come prepared to share some of your present thoughts with us next week. What is your conception of the ultimate reality of our existence that we call "God"? What personality do you ascribe to him? What do you dislike most about God? When you pray or worship, what mental picture of God do you have, if any?

What days, if any, did you miss daily Bible reading last week? What time of the day did you select for your reading?

NOTES:

[20]

Awareness
of
God

Experiment No. 2

THIS WEEK we begin our experiments in prayer. For some, it will be exciting and immediately rewarding. For many, it will be a slow process, demanding persistence and patience. God will come into our lives as soon as, but only when, we are ready for him to do so.

Prayer is a two-way street. There is a time to ask God's help through prayer, but there is also a time to open one-self to God as a morning glory opens itself to the sun, and await God's word. In this experiment, we are going to practice both attitudes.

First, set aside a definite time in each day for this exercise in prayer. Be disciplined enough to keep this appointment with God! At the beginning of this time, relax your body as thoroughly as you can. Spend two or three minutes con-sciously allowing muscles to relax—the face, neck, arms, hands, legs, feet—all in systematic order. Now you are ready to begin the practice of prayer.

Begin talking to God as you would any close friend. If it helps, direct your conversation with him to a chair or a bed. He is in the same room, not millions of miles off in space. Be free to talk informally and casually. God has a sense of humor too! Now, begin telling God how you see things as they shape up for the day. Tell him what you have to do

133

and how you feel toward it all. Be specific and to the point. If you would like some help in anything you have planned, tell him so. Tell him specifically what kind of help you need. Ask for that degree of specific help you have faith enough to believe he can furnish—"faith-sized" prayers. Get rid of all generalities!

Now that you have talked for awhile, it is time to listen. Relax your body again, in the same systematic way if necessary. Now, open to God's view all the hidden parts of your life. Let him know about every hidden area—the things you have done wrong, the things you are ashamed of, the places usually well-hidden, the pride, the falseness. Each day, look toward new areas, always being conscious of the actions of the previous day. Don't go back over ground already covered. You are now ready for God to communicate to you. Anticipate flash insights. The experience is much like receiving thought transfer. If your mind begins to wander, bring it back. Expect it to wander, but don't tolerate it. Prayer calls for more discipline than your daily work. Record the insights you receive.

Read the preceding two paragraphs of this experiment daily. Practice prayer faithfully, and come next week prepared to discuss the instructions you have received in this assignment, your own practice of prayer, and to share the results with the group.

NOTES:

[21]
Awareness
of
God

Experiment No. 3

LAST WEEK'S experiment in prayer was directed totally toward ourselves. This week we will begin to move into the exciting experience of seeing what our prayers can do for others.

In my experience, the most astounding answers to prayer have always come when the person or group praying had no stake whatsoever in what they were asking, nothing to gain. The prayer was totally unselfish and aimed toward others. This week's experiment will move in this directon.

You have two points in your present discipline of prayer. One is talking informally to God; the other is relaxed listening. Now add a third, and keep all three this week. Pray specifically and by name each day for each other member of your small group. Be specific! You will be humbled the first try by discovering how much you are asking for yourself and how hard it is to ask even one specific thing for another person you know well. Make this a part of your daily prayer discipline.

Now, another new experiment. Throughout any given week, we are present in many different situations that make us either feel victimized or helpless. This week try "spot prayer" in these moments. These are one-sentence prayers directed at a particular person on the spur of the moment.

Is the store cashier grouchy? Hit her with a quick one-sentence prayer. Not just a kind thought, but a concise sentence prayer that you say to yourself and to God. Does the gas man look tired? Hit him with a spot prayer. Does the person beside you in the restaurant look worried? Hit him or her with a spot prayer. Is a baby crying so loudly that no one in the theater can enjoy the movie? Try doing something about the situation with a spot prayer!!

Next week come prepared to discuss this experiment in spot prayer. Share the results. Pray, expecting results, and you will be dumbfounded at what happens.

NOTES:

[22]
Awareness
of
God

Experiment No. 4

How is your daily devotional Bible reading going? The first item of discussion next week is for each person in turn to report briefly on the time of day he has set aside for the experiments in Bible reading and prayer, the degree to which he has been able to discipline himself to observe it faithfully, and, in general, the results.

This week we are going to try to see "the image of God" in others. Be so aware of "the image of God" in them that you will treat them as Jesus treated persons.

Jesus very rarely, if ever, said an evil thing about another person. He did not look at people and immediately try to find fault. When he saw a person, he did not make a mental comparison of them with himself but looked always for "the image of God" in them. He saw them not as they were, but as God intended for them to be and as they could become. Thus, he was not reacting to the false fronts they put forth, but to the genuine persons God had made—persons they themselves were frequently unaware existed.

God does not want us to fashion others according to the image that seems good to us, that is, in our own image. Neither does he want us to copy the image that has seemed good to others to assume, that is, their own self-image. After all, even Jesus seemed a bit peculiar and eccentric to many

141

of us before we were able to see in him "the image of God." In that moment, it was not Jesus who was changed, but us!

Therefore, this week, control your tongue. Say nothing evil or unkindly critical about anyone. Say only positive things, good things. React to each person as he could be. By concentrating on the good in others, you will become aware that even the "worst" person is walking in the shadow of God.

NOTES:

[23]
Awareness
of
God

Experiment No. 5

THIS WEEK's experiment is the simplest of the series—and the hardest. It will take you only a moment, yet will take all your time.

This week we are going to become aware of what it is to be a disciple. All a disciple has to do is follow. It's a simple game of "follow the leader," but the leader is always taking unexpected twists and turns, and we're usually looking somewhere else when he does.

Discipleship is definitely not busy work! It is not thinking up things to do, even those "nice," "necessary," "Christian" things. It is an "availability" that takes concentrated effort and yet cannot be gained by training. The best, and in fact only, way to grasp discipleship is by practicing it daily. To be a disciple is to begin the experiment of playing follow the leader. Plan your own direction, however commendable, and you have quit playing the game—you are no longer a disciple!

This week, become aware of the number of opportunities to exercise action or understanding that God puts before you. Keep a careful running log for a week of the unexpected chances God gives you to make a real difference in the lives or environment of others. For example, I once thought, pending lab tests, that I had at the most only months to live. I wanted to talk it out with some Christian friends, but when I went to their house they were so busy "talking" that they didn't notice I was trying desperately to tell them something. Do we really listen? In another instance, I had changed a flat tire late at night. Upon finishing, I looked up to find a nearby resident had brought a pan of warm water, soap, and a towel for me to wash my dirty hands. I think his response was the sudden impulse of a disciple.

At first you will probably have a lot of hindsight observations. You will think of things you should have said or done differently. As the week progresses, become so aware of God-directed opportunities that you begin to react on the spur of the moment, by impulse. Dare to do and say things that you wouldn't if we were not involved in this experiment. Make these seven days one of the most fantastic adventures of your life. You may come to us next week as a totally new and different person, aware of God smack-dab in the center of your life!

NOTES:

[24]

Awareness
of
God

Experiment No. 6

DON'T FORGET to keep up the daily disciplines of Bible study and prayer. This week, add the pastor and the mission of your church to your daily prayers for others.

This week we are going to take positive steps toward being a witness to the fact that God makes a difference in the lives of men! We are going to dare to quote our own lives and the lives of others we love in our small group!

Jesus was very clear in his teaching that if you want to keep something, you have to give it away. This is at the heart of our own faith in God. I don't mean a fuzzy distant God, but the God who makes fantastic changes in the world we live in. Keep your faith to yourself and you will wake up some morning to find it has become meaningless. Keep trying to give it away and you'll find you're flooded with more than you know what to do with.

Be very clear on one point. We're not talking about the obligation or duty to "witness." We're not talking about assaulting the ears of others with words about how they can be converted and become better ("like us"?). We're talking about passing on some good news we have discovered because it was good news to us and we can't help wanting to share it—like passing on the word about a good movie or a good restaurant.

149

After I had seen the wonderful movie *Sound of Music*, I asked people for weeks if they had seen it. If they hadn't, I told them about how it had impressed me and how much I had enjoyed it. I even suggested that if they had the chance, they should see it themselves because I was sure they would enjoy it too! This is our pattern.

Our starting point and our whole approach this week will be our own group. Wonderful things have happened to us here. Why keep it a secret? We have learned that God really makes a difference! Each day try to tell at least one person about this group and quote a change you have seen in someone's life, hopefully your own (no quoting of what has been said in the group, of course). Be natural, relaxed, and casual. Don't talk as if you were trying to enlist them, but speak in confidence as one who has had a worthwhile and enjoyable experience you want to share. You're not trying to convince another that he would find something worthwhile—only relating how you have found something worthwhile.

Come next week and tell us about the people you have talked to and about their reactions. Note particularly whether or not the interest of the listener causes a natural progression from what the people in the group are doing to what God is doing in the group.

NOTES:

[25]

Awareness
of
God

Experiment No. 7

THIS IS THE last experiment in our twenty-four weeks to-gether. God has been deepening our fellowship and disciple-ship for six months. Now we are ready to leave the laboratory of experimentation behind and go into full-scale production! This group is ready to enter into God's mission for it!

We have casually acknowledged that the Church is the Body of Christ. Think on that a moment. Take it seriously. Christ has been resurrected. He has no flesh-and-blood body on this earth to perform the acts his mind plans and intends. He gives his orders to his new body, the Church. The Church provides the flesh-and-blood way of carrying out his wishes. Christ will change the world if his body will only carry out its part. That's us!

The Bible reminds us that the body is the sum of its parts. Some of us are one part, some another. Some are better feet for fast going, some stronger legs for tough climbing, some steadier hands for meticulous work, some clearer mouths for expression, and so on. No part is more valuable than another. To get the job done, each carries out the function it is best designed to carry out, in cooperation with the others doing likewise. Again, that's us!

Christ is leading us as a group into new missions. The

members of the group may change from time to time, but Christ has a challenge waiting for the group. This week, pray about this concept. Ask for a clear insight into the challenge he has prepared. Make a list of the potential missions that seem to be transferred into your own thinking. Come prepared to discuss your own readiness to be a component part of the Body of Christ and the clear challenges of mission possibilities that have come as answers to your own prayer.

NOTES:

[26]
Where
to
Now?

THE PERIOD OF guided experimentation is behind us. It is to be hoped that we have all become much more sensitive to our own feelings and more sure of our relationships with our fellow-men and God. We are members of a group within which we feel a high degree of confidence and with whom we desire to become part of the leaven making the Kingdom of God a reality on earth. Where do we go from here?

It is my hope that your small group can now see its place in God's scheme of things as a mission group. You may already have grasped a challenge that represents God's intention for you. You may choose to tackle it as a group or through individual members already professionally placed who need the unreserved support your group can offer. There is hardly a problem area in our world where an individual claiming to be Christian is not already at work. Such a person needs only the challenge to Christian mission and the guarantee of the support of the Christian community.

You may not yet recognize the mission in which your group can involve itself. It is possible that you have been insulated from some of the areas of God's creation that cry out for someone who cares. I suggest that you become aware of such needs through a set of living experiments of your own choosing. These could easily be called "Awareness of the World."

Make a list of those persons and agencies working in the areas of human misery and need about which you know little or nothing. Make arrangements to observe the operation of some of these agencies, and where possible, make appointments to meet with the persons responsible for their functioning at their places of employment. Simply tell them that you want to become better informed about their problems, and their doors will fly open to you! Such persons have a lot of groups who drop in to criticize, but few who are honestly concerned and desirous of learning more. You will want to make some visits as a group and some in groups of two or three. Among others that will come to mind, consider the following:

The mayor
The sheriff or police chief
Juvenile, traffic, or criminal court
City or county welfare director
A fire station
The emergency room of a hospital
A mental hospital or mental health clinic
A home for the aged
Red Cross facilities and blood bank

God works through his creation and with the persons he has created. There is no problem that does not contain within it the seeds for its resolution. Become an available and vulnerable creation of God. Learn something about the scope of his creation. When you find a problem that causes you to ask, "Why doesn't somebody do something about . . . ?" you may well hear the disturbing small voice of God ask, "Why don't you?"

48550